What people are

Peace or Pa

Liam Ó Ruairc's stated aim in this book is to present Irish republicanism as part of a wider, international struggle against oppression, injustice and exploitation. In exploring both the historical and contemporary forces that have shaped Irish politics he not only admirably succeeds in that project, but also challenges key aspects of the complacent consensus that has come to dominate public debate on both sides of the border since the late 1990s. By going beyond the mere repetition of worn out shibboleths Ó Ruairc's account reclaims the 'universal and emancipatory core' of republicanism and thus opens up new possibilities for political thought and action in Ireland.

Dr. Kevin Bean, Lecturer in Irish Politics, Institute of Irish Studies, University of Liverpool, author of *The New Politics of Sinn Féin* (2007)

Liam Ó Ruairc's Peace or Pacification? Northern Ireland After the Defeat of the IRA offers an interesting and provocative perspective on the Northern Ireland peace process. Neo-liberals who believe that there has been a "peace dividend" and those who believe that the "revolutionary ideology" of Irish Republicanism has been "de-republicanized" will benefit from Ó Ruairc's insightful presentation.

Robert W. White, Professor and Chair of the Department of Sociology at Indiana University-Purdue University Indianapolis (IUPUI), author of *Out of the Ashes: An Oral History of the Provisional Irish Republican Movement* (2017) and *Ruairí Ó Brádaigh: The Life and Politics of an Irish Revolutionary* (2006)

A fascinating and provocative book. Even those who remain unpersuaded by its arguments will benefit from engaging with it.

Richard English CBE (Commander of the British Empire), Fellow of the British Academy, Member of the Royal Irish Academy, Fellow of Royal Historical Society, Professor at and Pro-Vice-Chancellor Queen's University Belfast, author of *Armed Struggle: The History of the IRA* (2003), *Ernie O'Malley: IRA Intellectual* (1998)

Liam Ó Ruairc is one of the most fastidious commentators of the Irish political scene. Whether one agrees or disagrees with his opinion, his work is invariably scrupulously researched and supported evidentially. His book is, therefore, a welcome and valuable contribution to our understanding and analysis of the current political situation in the northern part of Ireland and deserves the wide readership that scholarship of this calibre merits.

Tommy McKearney, senior member of the Provisional IRA from the early 1970s until his arrest in 1977. Sentenced to life imprisonment, he served 16 years during which time he participated in the 1980 hunger strike in the Maze, author of: *The Provisional IRA: From Insurrection to Parliament* (2011)

Liam Ó Ruairc is a meticulous researcher with a particular eye for detail. A most astute observer of the Northern Irish political scene he has with this book brought acute discernment to major aspects of the peace process. This work will stand the test of time.

Anthony McIntyre, former IRA prisoner who spent eighteen years in the H-Blocks of Long Kesh prison, completed his PhD upon release and is the author of *Good Friday: The Death of Irish Republicanism* (2008)

Liam Ó Ruairc has written an important, revelatory analysis of the peace process in Northern Ireland which I am confident will take its place among the best books written about this consequential period in Anglo-Irish history. His underlying thesis is that what has happened in the near thirty years or so since the IRA recognized the southern state and embarked on a journey to constitutionalism is less a peace process and more a pacification process in which the republicans and the British co-operated to drain and enfeeble the vital ideological juices which had sustained resistance to partition for so long. The war in Ireland began with republicans and their allies abroad viewing the NI situation as a relic of British colonialism and ended with the militants accepting that it was really just a struggle over cultural identity; in the process republicans have been drained of their radicalism and now subscribe entirely to the neo-liberalism panacea. It is impossible to read this book and not wonder at the scale of the British triumph. The companion to this book, explaining how British intelligence so completely overwhelmed the IRA, has yet to be written. Until then Ó Ruairc's fine work will do very nicely.

Ed Moloney, former Northern Ireland editor for *The Irish Times* and *The Sunday Tribune*, author of: *A Secret History of the IRA* (2002; 2007), *Voices from the Grave: Two Men's War in Ireland* (2010)

Peace or Pacification?

Northern Ireland After the Defeat of the IRA

Peace or Pacification?

Northern Ireland After the Defeat of the IRA

Liam Ó Ruairc

Winchester, UK
Washington, USA

JOHN HUNT PUBLISHING

First published by Zero Books, 2019
Zero Books is an imprint of John Hunt Publishing Ltd., No. 3 East St., Alresford,
Hampshire SO24 9EE, UK
office@jhpbooks.net
www.johnhuntpublishing.com
www.zero-books.net

For distributor details and how to order please visit the 'Ordering' section on our website.

Text copyright: Liam Ó Ruairc 2018

ISBN: 978 1 78904 127 9
978 1 78904 128 6 (ebook)
Library of Congress Control Number: 2018946236

A CIP catalogue record for this book is available from the British Library.

Design: Stuart Davies

UK: Printed and bound by CPI Group (UK) Ltd, Croydon, CR0 4YY
US: Printed and bound by Thomson-Shore, 7300 West Joy Road, Dexter, MI 48130

We operate a distinctive and ethical publishing philosophy in
all areas of our business, from our global network of authors to
production and worldwide distribution.

Contents

Everybody knows that the dice are loaded
Everybody rolls with their fingers crossed
Everybody knows the war is over
Everybody knows the good guys lost
Everybody knows the fight was fixed
The poor stay poor, the rich get rich
That's how it goes
Everybody knows
Leonard Cohen (1988), Everybody Knows

A Brechtian maxim: 'Don't start from the good old things but the bad new ones.'
Walter Benjamin, Conversations with Brecht (diary notes), Svendborg, 25 August 1938

If there is anyone today to whom we can pass the responsibilities for the message we bequeath it is not to the 'masses', and not to the individual (who is powerless), but to an imaginary witness (eingebildeter Zeuge) – lest it perish with us.
Max Horkheimer and Theodor W. Adorno (1947), Dialektik der Aufklärung

Communists, when they are Marxists, and Marxists when they are Communists, never cry in the wilderness. Even when they are alone.
Louis Althusser (1973), Réponse à John Lewis

Presentation

For a good number of years, the Northern Irish 'peace process' has been sold abroad as a model for conflict resolution. The present study aims to show that this process is unable to ground 'peace' in 'justice' and that it is therefore more accurate to speak of a 'pacification process' than a peace process.

While dominant discourses reduce the so-called 'Irish Question' to an insular problem and ancestral hatreds, the present study grounds it in the context of colonialism, anti-imperialism and liberation struggles.

Its central argument is that the 'process' represents a major defeat for national liberation as it reinforces the partition of Ireland and that following the 1998 Agreement, Sinn Féin has become a junior partner of the British state.

The 'peace process' also has an economic aspect according to which neo-liberal social and economic policies are the best way to consolidate peace. This study shows that the economic side of the peace process has only increased social and economic inequalities and that the people who were affected the most by the conflict are those who benefit the least from so-called 'peace dividends'.

The peace process is placed in the context of the 'end of history' thesis proclaimed by Fukuyama and the defeat of what was called 'actually existing socialism' in general and 'actually existing national liberation movements' in particular. It is this international context which made the process possible. Despite its defeat, this study is seeking to maintain the universal and emancipatory content of Irish republicanism.

It is based on what is most serious and advanced on the subject, many university journals the general reader is probably not familiar with. The many references to those publications in this study are to encourage the reader to look up those references

1

and become familiar with their content.

The author would like to develop for the Northern Irish situations analyses similar to those made in the context of Palestine by Edward W. Said, Noam Chomsky, Ilan Pappé, Joseph A. Massad and Norman Finkelstein. This study certainly shares their values and has an 'affiliation' with those of Edward W. Said in particular.

Said noted he desired 'a connection between Fanon and Adorno that is totally missing': 'In other words, activism, nationalism, revolution, insurrection on the one hand, and on the other, the excessive kind of theoretical reflection and speculation of the sort one associates with the Frankfurt school...' In that spirit this study aspires to 'thinking about the future in ways that are not simply insurrectionary or reactive[1]'.

Liam Ó Ruairc, 4 July 2018

---

1   Edward W. Said (2004), *Power, Politics and Culture: Interviews with Edward W. Said*, London: Bloomsbury, 51

Part One. Insular problem or universal cause?

You must remember that the cause of human freedom is as wide as the world.
Roger Casement, Letter to E.D. Morel, 8 April 1911

I am so grateful to Ireland...You have had many more years of imperialism than we have had, and you have produced a fabulous culture of resistance and an extraordinary spirit, which I desperately hope we (the Palestinian people) can measure up to by about 10 per cent...There are three places that have meant a great deal to me; one is South Africa, another is Ireland, and the third is India. These places have meant a great deal to me culturally, not just because there was always a spirit of resistance, but because out of it, there is this huge cultural effort which I think is much more important than arms, and armed struggle.
Edward W. Said, Interview with Kevin Whelan, Dublin, 24 June 1999

Peace process

The term 'peace process' in the context of Northern Ireland refers to a series of major political developments since the early 1990s. It is the process that led to the IRA ceasefire in 1994, the negotiations that led to the 1998 Agreement, and all subsequent developments until former adversaries agreed to share power in 2007. All these developments have laid the foundations of where Northern Ireland is politically today. The 'peace process' is generally presented as a success and a model to emulate in other conflict zones elsewhere in the world. In 2018, researchers for the University of Edinburgh set up a database called PA-X (Peace Agreement Access Tool) recording more than 140 peace processes which have produced more than 1,500 agreements aimed at

3

resolving conflicts between 1990 and 2015, demonstrating the lasting impact of the Irish peace process on subsequent agreements worldwide[1]. For governments, the process shows how 'talking to terrorists' can lead to historic compromises. For insurgents it is an example of why governments should dialogue with them and negotiate a solution. It is those references to the Northern Irish model and the proposal to emulate it that makes it a politically relevant issue. The Northern Irish 'model' is, however, not well understood if not misunderstood and makes a critical analysis all the more imperative.

Before developing this critical analysis, this chapter will first explain why and how Northern Ireland was created as a political entity, and the nature of the conflict that was its consequence. It will show that this is not just some 'insular' problem but that it has global significance, making it politically relevant. It will outline the political perspective from which this analysis is written, and will attempt to show what is truly universal in it, as well as its democratic content. But beforehand, one should warn the reader of the fundamental problem that the 'peace process' is in open conflict with the notion of truth, and remind them of the importance of truth in politics.

Truth or 'constructive ambiguity'?

One of the problems with the media coverage of the Northern Ireland situation is that the conflict generated a real 'information war'. The boundaries between information and disinformation, analysis and propaganda were very thin. Censorship, lies and media manipulation were common in this 'propaganda war' in which the British state was the main actor.[2] The media generally adopted the perspective of the British government on the conflict and gave the republican perspective a hostile treatment. Republicans never had the means that were available to the British state and had a marginal impact in terms of putting their message across. In this context, developing an alternative perspective on the conflict reaching a wide audience is very difficult. Has the peace process ended this 'information war'? Did it reduce lies and manipulations in the media? The answer is negative, as the symbiosis between media and the state continued and the war propaganda has been replaced by what media experts called 'the propaganda of peace'[3]. For example, *Information Strategy*, a British government document written by Tom Kelly, formerly of the BBC and Director of Communications at the Northern Ireland Office at the time of the 1998 Agreement, outlines the government's strategy for getting the right result through a campaign of blatant media manipulation designed to flood Northern Ireland with positive stories about the peace deal[4]. Government spin has been reinforced by the reluctance of the media to ask critical questions. The media has been accused by award-winning journalist Ed Moloney of covering up the truth to protect the peace process and being reluctant to report events unhelpful to the peace process. Before journalists were reluctant to question the official line afraid of being called 'terrorist sympathisers', today out of fear of being labelled 'JAPPs' – 'journalists against the peace process'. If official censorship ended in 1994, self-censorship by the media has in fact increased since[5]. Moreover, there are 160 press officers in Stormont – more than there are journalists in Belfast newsrooms – and newspapers are struggling to do anything other than copy and paste their press releases[6]. By 2007, most international media no longer had any permanent presence in Northern Ireland, leaving the public abroad even less informed of the situation there[7]. In 2007, Bernadette McAliskey and award-winning playwright Gary Mitchell (who was forced to leave Belfast with his extended family due to Loyalist hostility at his plays) expressed strong criticism of the media's coverage of the peace process. In Mitchell's view there is a 'real truth' and an 'agreed truth', and when the 'agreed truth becomes accepted, the real truth becomes a lie'. The media is reporting the agreed truth and the real truth 'doesn't get a look in', he argued. A major reason for this, according to Bernadette McAliskey, is that with the complicity of the media and through spin and choreography, peace has been bought by 'perjury, fraud, corruption, cheating and lying[8]'.

The creation and maintenance of both the peace process and the 1998 Agreement have been judged to involve lying and deception. Twenty years after 1998 Professor Paul Dixon concluded that the 'inconvenient truth' about the Belfast Agreement 'is that, if it wasn't for deliberate deceptions, there would be no peace process[9]'. Former British Prime Minister Tony Blair admits lying to further the process[10]. Former republican leader and hunger striker Brendan Hughes complained that 'the process had created a class of professional liars and unfortunately it contains many Republicans[11]'. Thanks to the peace process it now seems that 'lying for Ireland' has replaced 'dying for Ireland'. Much more serious it is now argued that the very idea of truth is unhelpful to the peace process and that lies are morally justified if they help to advance it. There are supposed to be 'honourable' and 'dishonourable' deceptions. Spin, lying and manipulation were essential to move the process forward[12]. Central to the process is not the idea of 'truth' but rather that of 'constructive ambiguity'[13]. As prominent Sinn Féin member Jim Gibney reminds us: 'If there is one big lesson coming out of the peace process...it is words like 'certainty' and 'clarity' are not part of the creative lexicon that conflict resolution requires if it is to be successful...Give me the language of ambiguity...It has oiled the engine of the peace process. Long may it continue to do so[14].' In a more global context of peace processes from Palestine to South Africa, Noam Chomsky notes that 'a whole new vocabulary has been designed to disguise reality': in this Orwellian language, 'peace process' does not refer to the process of seeking peace but to the political initiatives of dominant powers, 'making peace' means accepting the terms of the US and its allies, 'pragmatists' and 'moderates' are those who accept them, whereas 'extremists' and 'hardliners' are those who don't[15]. Roy Foster was right to conclude that 'the British quickly learned linguistic ingenuity; Orwell would have appreciated the way an 'agreed Ireland' turned out to mean the very opposite of a 'united Ireland', while 'power-sharing' came to denote 'separate spheres', not reconciliation[16]. Such a context of 'propaganda of peace', of deliberate lies and 'creative ambiguity' makes an analysis demythologising the peace process all the more urgent. To use an expression attributed to George Orwell: 'In times of universal deceit, telling the truth is a revolutionary act.'

Partition

Since being set up at the beginning of the 1920s, Northern Ireland has been the subject of recurring political conflict. It is necessary to recall the nature of this conflict, that the media sometimes wrongly present as a religious war, and more often as a problem of two deeply divided communities that have problems with each other. The origin of this conflict lies in the British state's refusal to recognise the right of the people of Ireland as a whole to self-determination, for which it had massively voted in 1918. As early as 1916, Prime Minister Lloyd George wrote to unionist leader Lord Carson: 'We must make it clear that Ulster does not, whether she wills it or not, merge with the rest of Ireland[17].' In 1921 Carson bitterly concluded: 'What a fool I was! I was only a puppet, and so was Ulster, and so was Ireland, in the political game that was to get the Conservative Party into power...[18]'

'Northern Ireland' was imposed by the British state, not created by the will of the people of Ireland who had massively voted for all-Ireland independence in 1918. British Prime Minister Lloyd George was to admit in 1921: 'If you asked the people of Ireland what plan they would accept, by an emphatic majority they would say: "We want independence and an Irish Republic." There is absolutely no doubt about that[19].' Northern

Ireland was established by a 1920 British Act of Parliament for which no one in Ireland ever voted: the Government of Ireland Act which became law on 23 December 1920 and the division of the island into two distinct jurisdictions took place on 3 May 1921, more than 6 months prior to the 1921 treaty. The people of all Ireland were given no say on the matter.

The partition of Ireland is not even based on the wishes of the people within the partitioned area. Along the actual border, areas were included where the majority wished to be on the other side of the line. There are even some indications that the unionists did not want partition[20]. Unionist leader Edward Carson himself said: 'Ulster asks for no separate Parliament. She never has, in all the long controversy, taken that course[21].' As late as 1919 Edward Carson told the House of Commons: 'I cannot understand why we should ask them to take a Parliament which they never demanded and which they do not want...I know Ulster does not want this Parliament[22].' Some historians argue that some sort of partition was inevitable. However, it was the British government which chose the way in which Ireland was to be divided and imposed this by force. It is inconceivable that negotiations between republicans, nationalists and unionists would have produced the same settlement, especially had the British state been out of the equation. The primary responsibility for partition lies with the British government and Northern Ireland is kept in existence only by British guns and finance.

It is sometimes argued that partition was legitimate because a majority in what became Northern Ireland wished to remain part of the United Kingdom. But one has to draw a line where the majority for partition begins and where the majority for partition ends. The only recognised constitutional entity until 1920 was the 32-county Ireland until the British government over-ruled the democracy of Ireland and split the country. It was governed as an entity for 750 years under English rule. Lloyd George, who was to become British Prime Minister, said:

Take all the great questions through years of controversy in Ireland and in this country, during the last twenty or thirty years, or even beyond that, and in regard to all those questions it will be found that Ireland has been treated as a whole, as a separate unit, and there has never been a demand from any county in Ireland or from any part of Ireland or from any party in Ireland that Ulster should be treated separately.

In the same speech he described the proposal to exclude part of Ireland from Irish self-government as 'a gigantic demand which would be a serious departure from every precedent[23]'. Interestingly the unionist leader Edward Carson more than once stressed the fact that Ireland was an indivisible unit, though he wanted to keep it under the Imperial Parliament.: 'the only way you can treat Ireland, having regard to her special conditions, is to treat her as one entity by the Imperial Parliament, and the moment you try to alter that, the idea of governing Ireland with anything like peace falls away[24]'. There are therefore serious grounds to take the 32-county Ireland as being the legitimate unit for self-determination. However, the historical, geographical or national bases to justify the existence of Northern Ireland are more questionable. The six-county Northern Ireland is not the nine-county Ulster and there is little that makes its population distinctive from the rest of the island (also not all Protestants in Ulster consider themselves to be British or unionists). To take Northern Ireland as a legitimate unit for self-determination has little political, geographic or historic logic[25]. Interestingly in September 2017 European Parliament Brexit chief Guy Verhofstadt stated the Irish border was in no way a natural one, it was not a river, nor a mountain range. 'It meanders for 310 miles through meadows, forests, farmlands,' he said. Visiting a border farm in county Monaghan, he remarked that it was impossible to see where one jurisdiction begins and the other ends. Mr Verhofstadt described the border as an 'illogical divide' and called for it to remain invisible. 'Certainly the cows couldn't see it. Cows from the North eating grass from the South, milked in the North by a farmer from the South with their milk bottled in the South,' he said. 'I'm a Belgian so surrealism comes naturally to me, but to reinstate the border would be more than surreal, it would be totally absurd, even for me[26].' In 1920, British Prime Minister Lloyd George warned unionist leader Lord Craigavon on partition: 'Your proposal would stereotype a frontier based neither on national features nor broad geographical considerations, by giving it the character of an international boundary. Partition on those grounds the majority of the Irish people will never accept, neither could we conscientiously attempt to enforce it.[27]' For British Prime Minister Asquith 'Ireland is a nation; not two nations, but one nation.[28]'He also said: 'You can no more split Ireland into parts than you can split England or Scotland into parts[29].' For Winston Churchill: 'I am not at all prepared to admit that there are two nations in Ireland. I look upon the Irish nation as one people[30].' Referring to the unionist minority's use of the threat of partition to defeat the proposal to give Ireland self-government, Winston Churchill said: 'On one point I think there will be very little dispute: Whatever Ulster's right may be, she cannot stand in the way of the whole of the rest of Ireland. Half a province cannot impose a permanent veto on the nation[31].' Ramsay MacDonald, who was later to become Prime Minister of the United Kingdom, also emphasised the essential unity of Ireland and questioned the right of the unionist minority to impede the progress of a nation: 'The first question is: Is Ulster to deny the rights of the rest of Ireland to self-government? We say: "No, emphatically not!" Arising out of that, and a somewhat narrower question, is this: Is Ulster going to deny the right of Ireland ever to speak and act and govern itself as a united nationality? We say "No, emphatically not![32]"' Finally, the aggregate verdict is the normal means of assessing an electoral contest so even if a 'majority' in the North wished to remain part of the United Kingdom this lacked democratic legitimacy.

In fact 'Northern Ireland' did not demand self-determination, it was created to deny self-determination. 'Northern Ireland' was created and maintained through the threat of violence and denial of democracy. Its origin was a sectarian headcount as John Whyte explains:

> For the border was so drawn as to corral within it not only almost all areas with unionist majorities, but also considerable areas with nationalist ones. If the county is taken as the unit, there were at the time of partition unionist majorities in only four of the six counties of Northern Ireland. If some smaller unit had been chosen then parts of Tyrone and Fermanagh might have been reclaimed for unionism, but considerable parts of other counties would have been lost to nationalism... (Unionists') only worry was how much territory they would be able to control. The idea that it might be unjust to ask for more territory than was actually unionist apparently never entered their heads. The fact might be used by their critics to argue that unionists sought, not equality, but supremacy[33].

On that basis, one can seriously challenge the idea of Bew, Gibbon and Patterson, a group of prominent political scientists and historians, that 'there is nothing inherently reactionary about...a national frontier which puts Protestants in numerical majority[34]'.

As a result of this the people of Ireland were denied their rights as a majority and an undemocratic system of artifical majority and artificial minority was set up. What made partition 'legitimate' was that a majority in the North wanted it when partition had created this majority in the first place, making it artificial. Critics say those who claim 'there was something *artificial* about the creation of Northern Ireland' imply 'that there was something more *natural* about a non-partitioned Ireland[35]'. However: 'There is much to substantiate the Irish nationalist claim...that the administrative boundaries of the Irish colonial state constituted the obvious *historical* (not natural) unit within which the exercise of self-determination should be decided[36].'

Since democracy is usually equated with majority rule, many would argue that it would be undemocratic to force the unionists, who are now a majority in Northern Ireland, into a united Ireland without their consent. What this argument ignores is precisely the artificial nature of this 'majority'. Prior to partition unionists constituted a minority within the whole population of Ireland. The very existence of Northern Ireland is due to the British government and unionists' refusal to accept the results of majority rule in Ireland as a whole. To attempt to legitimise that refusal unionists had to be transformed into a 'majority'. This was achieved by creating 'Northern Ireland' whose borders were deliberately chosen to exclude counties which were predominantly nationalist and republican. In this new state unionists thus enjoyed a clear majority. The fact that within Northern Ireland unionists can outvote nationalists and republicans is simply an outcome of the way in which its borders were fixed at the time of partition and says nothing about the justice or democratic nature of their case. The principle of consent for constitutional change only refers to consent within the six counties against the will of the majority of the people of Ireland and has therefore questionable democratic credentials.

The year 2021 will mark 100 years since Northern Ireland was established and this section tried to show that its very concept was democratically flawed. The republican case against partition and the existence of Northern Ireland is not a matter of 'irredentism', it is fundamentally an issue of democracy. For republicans the problem is first and foremost that 'Northern Ireland' is a product of gerrymandering and not democracy. It is based on a sectarian headcount to maintain supremacy, not equality. It is not based on consent but on coercion. And as will be showed now, it is not based upon the 'rule of law' but on a system where normal rules of justice can be circumvented.

Land of Habeas Corpus or state of exception?

Unionists benefited from a clear majority within Northern Ireland. There were about 65 per cent of unionists (the majority of them from a Protestant background) for around 35 per cent of nationalists and republicans (the majority of them from a Catholic background). The fact that the unionists were a majority was simply a consequence of how the border had been drawn and does not prove the democratic content of their position. As *The Sunday Times Insight Team* noted: 'The border was itself the first and biggest gerrymander: the six counties it enclosed, the new province of Ulster, had no point or meaning except as the largest area which the Protestant tribe could hold against the Catholic. Protestant supremacy was the only reason why the State existed. As such, the State was an immoral concept. It therefore had to be maintained from the first by immoral means[37].'

The artificial majority set about building (in the words of Unionist Prime Minister Craig on 24 April 1934) 'a Protestant state for a Protestant people', a state built on discrimination and bigotry. While 'Northern Ireland' was formally democratic, as an entity where more than a third of its population contested its legitimacy, it could not function as a normal democratic state. From the moment of its birth, Northern Ireland has been in a state of more or less continuous emergency where civil liberties have been severely curtailed. Many civil liberties taken for granted in other Western countries have always been severely restricted in the six counties. In 1936 the National Council for Civil Liberties commented that the Unionists had created 'under the shadow of the British constitution a permanent machine of dictatorship' and compared Northern Ireland with the fascist dictatorships then current in Europe; and in April 1963, B. J.

Vorster, then Justice Minister and future President of South Africa, commented that he would be willing to exchange all the apartheid legislation for only one of the repressive laws existing in Northern Ireland[38]. Northern Ireland was an exceptional state relying on special powers, sectarianism and electoral fraud for its survival. Nationalists became an artificial minority and were long treated as second-class citizens. The Irish socialist James Connolly had predicted that partition would generate a 'carnival of reaction' and he was proved right.

The United Kingdom is a constitutional monarchy and a formally democratic state, how does one explain that in the country of Habeas Corpus such an exceptional regime in Northern Ireland was possible? From the moment of its foundation, emergency legislation was central to the governing of Northern Ireland. In a 'normal' parliamentary democracy based on 'the rule of law', where there is a relative consensus on the legitimacy of the state and government institutions, emergency legislation is introduced in situations of crisis. Set up because of exceptional circumstance, the state of emergency is of a temporary nature. If in theory parliamentary democracies return to the 'rule of law' once the crisis is over, in the case of Northern Ireland – where the legitimacy of the state is challenged by a substantial portion of the population – this is not possible and emergency legislation becomes permanent. This is where one can see the limits of the argument made by some[39] that the most reprehensible aspects of the Northern Ireland political entity are not a necessary consequence of partition but only the regrettable product of a particular form of administration. Under the Act of Union from 1800-1921, the British government brought in 105 Coercion Acts dealing with Ireland. That means that Habeas Corpus was as often suspended as in force in nineteenth-century Ireland. These Coercion Acts survived, along with various forms of legalised discrimination, in the form of emergency legislation in Northern Ireland. Emergency legislation from the Civil Authorities

(Special Powers) Act (1922) to the Northern Ireland (Emergency Provisions) Act (1973) and its subsequent versions, and the Prevention of Terrorism (Temporary Provisions) Act (1974) have been a constant since 1921 even in periods of peace[40]. To use their official name, the 'special', 'emergency' and 'temporary' nature of these laws show their exceptional nature. The fact that these 'special', 'emergency' and 'temporary' legislations have lasted for decades with little parliamentary debate shows that the state of emergency has become permanent[41].

The United Kingdom has the dubious distinction of being the European state judged to have been the most consistent violator of human rights throughout the 1970s and 1980s. During this period the UK government had more cases taken against it under the European Convention on Human Rights than any other country, and has had more adverse judgements made against it than any other country. The vast majority of the accusations, and associated rulings, have been in relation to the British state's handling of the conflict in Northern Ireland and the state of emergency there. Concerns about human rights violations in Northern Ireland have been voiced by the United Nations High Commissioner for Human Rights, the UNHCHR's Sub-Commission on the Promotion and Protection of Human Rights, the Human Rights Committee and Committee Against Torture as well as the Council of Europe's European Committee for the Prevention of Torture. Human rights abuses in Northern Ireland have also been the subject of criticisms from a range of international NGOs, including Amnesty International, Human Rights Watch, the Lawyers Committee for Human Rights and Statewatch, as well as from human rights groups based in Northern Ireland. Concerns have been raised about the use, by the Royal Ulster Constabulary (RUC) and the British Army, of 'shoot-to-kill' squads, of collusion between the security forces and Loyalist paramilitaries in the killing of Irish Nationalists (including the killing of prominent human rights lawyers) and the army and RUC's use of torture on detainees. The RUC has also come in for criticism for its excessive use of force in policing, including its use of plastic bullet rounds against children. The judicial system has been criticised for its draconian emergency legislation, including extensive powers of detention, the use of uncorroborated evidence from informers to convict suspected insurgents, and a two-tier justice system in which jury-less courts are used for those accused of 'scheduled' (i.e. political) offences[42]. These controversial practices of the British state in Northern Ireland are no accident but are a direct product of this permanent state of emergency[43]. What Giorgio Agamben called 'the state of exception as a paradigm of government' directly applies to the situation in Northern Ireland[44]. The human rights problems within Northern Ireland predate the recent conflict and have afflicted the province since its creation. Therefore, it is correct to conclude that in Northern Ireland 'political violence was a symptom rather than the cause of *state pathology*[45]'.

'Troubles' or war?

According to official British statistics, in the six counties between 1969 and 1998 there were some 35,669 shooting incidents and 10,412 explosions; 11,483 firearms and 115,427 kilos of explosives were seized during 359,699 searches, from 1972 some 18,258 were charged with scheduled offences, and some 3289 people were killed and another 42,216 injured as a result of the conflict in the North[46]. Brendan O'Leary and John McGarry point out that 'nearly two per cent of the population of Northern Ireland have been killed or injured through political violence', a figure close to 1 in 50 of the population: 'If the equivalent ratio of victims to population had been produced in Great Britain in the same period some 100,000 people would have died, and if a similar level of political violence had taken place, the number of fatalities in the USA would have been over 500,000, or about ten times the number of Americans killed in the Vietnam war.' It is legitimate to classify the conflict as a 'war', 'the Irish euphemism for the conflict, "the Troubles", is just that: a euphemism'[47]. The human cost is high. Some 7000 parents have thus lost a child, some 14,000 grandparents a grandchild. An estimated 3000 people have lost a spouse, affecting around 10,000 children, while perhaps 15,000 have lost a sibling. Some 45,000 may have lost an uncle or aunt and around 21,000 a niece or nephew. All in all, more than 115,000 people may have lost a close relative[48].

Of the 3747 people killed as a result of the conflict between 1966 and 2006, the book *Lost Lives* breaks them down into the following categories:

Catholic Civilians: 1259 (33.6 per cent)
Security Forces: 1039 (27.7 per cent)
Protestant Civilians: 727 (19.4 per cent)
Republican Activists: 395 (10.5 per cent)
Loyalist Activists: 167 (4.4 per cent)
Others-Unknown: 160 (4.2 per cent)

(David McKittrick, Seamus Kelters, Brian Feeney and Chris Thornton, *Lost Lives: The stories of the men, women and children who died as a result of the Northern Ireland troubles*, Edinburgh: Mainstream Publishing Company, Revised and updated edition, 2007, p.1555)

It should be noted that approximately 20 per cent of Protestant civilians killed were murdered by Loyalists because they were mistaken for Catholics. These casualty figures demonstrate that the two largest categories of fatalities were 'Catholic Civilians' killed by the security forces and Loyalists, and members of the security forces killed by republicans. The largest category of deaths is Catholic civilians. Statistically they were those most at risk of death in the conflict. To put these deaths in context, Catholics represent one-third of the population of the North but suffered nearly three-fifths of the civilian casualties. 'Catholic civilians have evidently suffered both absolutely and relatively more than Protestant civilians[49].' The number of Catholics killed per 1000 of population was 2.48 and Protestants 1.46. Catholics were at approximately 50 per cent greater risk of being killed, both relatively and absolutely.

While it should be noted that 'neither community in Northern Ireland has a monopoly of suffering in the present conflict, among both Catholics and Protestants, hundreds have been killed and thousands injured, lives have been ruined and homes wrecked', it should be emphasised that: 'In relative terms it is undoubtedly the Catholics who have suffered the most, for it is against them that the main weight of repression has been directed. Most of the vast number of people imprisoned over the years for so-called 'terrorist' (i.e. political) offences have been Catholics and most of the victims of sectarian assassinations have also been Catholics[50].'

A study carried out by the University of Ulster on the 3593 conflict-related deaths between 1969 and 1998 estimated that 1543 of the dead were Catholics, including 355 republican activists. In terms of agencies responsible for those 1543 deaths:

Killed by Loyalists: 735 (47.6 per cent)
Killed by Republicans: 381 (24.7 per cent)
Killed by Security Forces: 316 (20.5 per cent)
Others-Unknown: 111 (7.2 per cent)

(Source: Marie Therese Fay, Mike Morrissey and Marie Smyth, *Mapping Troubles-Related Deaths in Northern Ireland 1969-1998*, INCORE (University of Ulster and The United Nations University), Second edition with amendments reprinted 1998, Table 1.1 Deaths by Religion by Organisation Responsible)

'Killed by Republicans' includes 95 IRA volunteers killed in accidental or premature explosions as well as 12 hunger strikers, which explains why that category is higher than killed by security forces. These statistics show that there were two campaigns of violence in the North, the republican war against the British state, and the security forces and Loyalist paramilitaries counter-insurgency campaign not just against republicans but against the Catholic population as a whole. Civilian deaths constitute the largest category of victims of state killings – over 50 per cent. Almost all such victims were unarmed; the vast majority – 86 per cent – were Catholic. The next largest category is republican activists, accounting for 37 per cent of state killings. Remarkably few Loyalist paramilitaries were victims of state killings – only 4 per cent of the total. If it is presumed as a shorthand calculation that republican activists were likely to have been Catholic while Loyalist activists were likely to have been Protestant, it follows that the Catholic or nationalist community experienced the overwhelming bulk of killing by state forces; 88 per cent of victims of state killings were from the nationalist community.

Deaths resulting from collusion between state forces and Loyalist paramilitary groups are not included in the above figures. 'To do so would be to add at least the same number of deaths again.' Collusion has been a factor in Loyalist killings since early in the conflict, but reached a peak in the early 1990s. As Arthur Fegan and Raymond Murray documented, between March 1990 and September 1994, Loyalists killed 185 people. Of these deaths, 168 (91 per cent) were sectarian or political in nature, and in 103 cases (56 per cent of all the Loyalist killings in the period) there is evidence of some form of collusion[51].

Roy Greenslade, a former editor of *The Daily Mirror* working today for *The Guardian*, has noted the media's tendency to create a 'hierarchy of deaths' in which those killed by republicans receive the most coverage while those killed by Loyalists the least. Those forming the largest single category of fatalities are thus actually the most invisible in the media[52]. The 'hierarchy of deaths' is most visible when looking how the media covered the deaths of children during the conflict. Between 1969 and 1998, 23 children under 5 years of age, 24 between 6 and 11, and 210 aged between 12 and 17 were killed as a result of political violence. Security forces and Loyalists are responsible for the majority of the killings (67 and 74) and republicans for 90 (some of them soldiers not yet 18 years of age)[53]. Yet this has not been reflected in media coverage. There are 'deserving' and 'undeserving' victims.

The media, however, often points out that civilians and non-combatants constitute the largest category of victims of the conflict, but without specifying this important fact:

Civilian Victims from Political Violence, 1969-1998:
Civilian Deaths as Percentage of Deaths by this Agency:
Loyalists: 87.2 per cent
Security Forces: 54.4 per cent
Republicans: 35.6 per cent

(Calculated on the basis of Marie Therese Fay, Mike Morrissey and Marie Smyth, Mapping *Troubles-Related Deaths in Northern Ireland 1969-1998*, INCORE (University of Ulster and The United Nations University), Second edition with amendments reprinted 1998, Table 1.2 Political Status of Victims by Organisations Responsible for Deaths)

The war in the North is often reduced by the media to 'terrorism'. In the case of terrorism, there is no agreed definition in international law, nor is there consensus among scholars; and moreover the term is politically contested. There have been numerous diplomatic efforts aimed at producing an agreed definition of terrorism. The formula which many governments and international organisations have decided to adopt describes terrorism as politically motivated violence that intentionally targets civilians and non-combatants. This approach has been adopted in various United Nations Security Council Resolutions dealing with terrorism and was endorsed by the UN Secretary General in March 2005[54]. On the basis of this definition and the statistics above, one would be unable to label unequivocally republicans as terrorists – they have actually been the most discriminate party to the conflict – but on the other hand the security forces would qualify as terrorists since a majority of their casualties are civilians. On top of that it is difficult to present the conflict as one between 'terrorism' and 'law and order'. An investigation for example showed that members of the British Army Ulster Defence Regiment were one and a half times more likely to be convicted of scheduled offences than the adult civilians whom they were supposed to be protecting[55].

An insular problem?

What is the global significance of the Northern Ireland problem? Some would say that the best point of comparison would be territorial and 'ethnic frontier' disputes in Europe such as Schleswig-Holstein, the Åland Islands, Trentino-Alto Adige/ Südtirol or Upper Silesia for example[56]. But what this misses is that the question of the partition of Ireland is not some local and insular problem, but part of a global trend of conflict between imperialism and anti-imperialism. For Edward W. Said, Ireland 'is the major European colony'[57]. Said noted elsewhere that while the Irish struggle was a 'model of twentieth-century wars of liberation', 'it is an amazing thing that the problem of Irish liberation not only has continued longer than other comparable struggles, but is so often not regarded as being an imperial or nationalist issue; instead it is comprehended as an aberration within the British dominions. Yet the facts conclusively reveal otherwise[58].' The idea that Ireland (or one of its parts) is or has been a 'colony' at some stage remains very controversial[59]. Even if the country is geographically located in Europe and has been constitutionally part of the United Kingdom metropolis since 1801, there are solid grounds to analyse Ireland's position within a context of imperial domination[60]. From 1801 Ireland became an integral part of the United Kingdom with parliamentary representation, but unlike England, Wales and Scotland, Westminster continued to govern the country until 1925 through the Colonial Office, not the Home Office[61]. Policing in Ireland was not only different from the rest of the UK but the Irish constabulary 'model' provided the model for policing colonies, indicating its colonial nature[62]. Yet most analyses do not give sufficient weight to this colonial dimension.

The movement for Irish self-determination was part of the rise of anti-colonial nationalisms[63]. Irish republicans supported the national liberation movements in India and Egypt for example, the same way Ho Chi Minh and others identified with the struggle of the Irish people[64]. This has been particularly documented by studies for the case of India[65]. Irish republicans saw their struggle in a broader anti-imperialist context and not simply a nationalist one. In their own words, their struggle was against 'the British Empire...the crucifixion of India and the degradation of Egypt[66]'. It was an essential part of their politics which had a fundamentally democratic and progressive content. If the Irish are 'white', one must mention the remarkable influence that their struggle had on racially subaltern groups. If Ireland already interested Frederick Douglass or W.E.B Du Bois, according to Marcus Garvey the republican struggle in Ireland has a larger impact on the Universal Negro Improvement Association than anti-imperialist struggles in India, China or Egypt[67]. For historian Eric Hobsbawm, decolonisation was one of the chief advances of the 'short twentieth century', and a key achievement of the struggle which began with the 1916 Easter Rising is to have accelerated this process. In his foreword to Frantz Fanon's book *The Wretched of the Earth*, Jean-Paul Sartre noted, 'Not so very long ago, the earth numbered two thousand million inhabitants: five hundred million men and women, and two thousand five hundred million natives[68].' The Irish struggle's lasting contribution is to hasten the process through which 'natives' became fully 'men and women'. Interestingly the April 1972 edition of *An Phoblacht*, the official newspaper of the Irish Republican Movement, reported that a petition had been circulated in France, the signatories 'associating themselves with the international campaign launched by the resistance organisations in Northern Ireland'. Signatories included Jean-Paul Sartre and Simone de Beauvoir.

Leading establishment figures saw Ireland as a vital link in the chain that bound the British Empire together, so to lose Ireland would mean to lose the Empire. 'If we lose Ireland we have lost the Empire,' declared Chief of the Imperial General Staff and Field-Marshal Sir Henry Wilson on 30 March 1921[69]. On 14 December 1921 in the House of Lords, unionist leader Edward Carson warned the British government of the consequences of defeat in Ireland for the Empire: 'If you tell your Empire in India, in Egypt, and all over the world that you do not got the men, the money, the pluck, the inclination and the backing to restore order in a country within twenty miles of your own shore, you may as well begin to abandon the attempt to make British rule prevail throughout the Empire at all[70].' In response to the Irish demand for independence, British Prime Minister David Lloyd George told his cabinet in Inverness on 7 September 1921: 'Suppose we gave it to them? It will lower the prestige and the dignity of this country and reduce British authority to a low point in Ireland itself. It will give the impression that we have lost grip, that the Empire has no further force and will have an effect on India and throughout Europe[71].' From an opposite point of view, in his defence of the 1916 Irish insurrection, Lenin had similarly underlined its explosive political effects:

The struggle of the oppressed nations in Europe, a struggle

capable of going to the length of insurrection and street fighting, of breaking down the iron discipline in the army and martial law will sharpen the revolutionary crisis in Europe infinitely more than a much more developed rebellion in a remote colony. A blow delivered against British imperialist bourgeois rule by a rebellion in Ireland is of a hundred times greater political significance than a blow of equal weight in Asia or in Africa[72].

The British state's decision to partition Ireland has not to be understood purely in an Irish context; but in the overall context of its Empire. The British Empire's determination to meet the challenge from Ireland as exemplified by the Easter Rising led to the partition of the country. King George V had reminded Ulster MPs at the first opening of the Northern Ireland Parliament that 'everything that touches Ireland finds an echo in the remotest part of the Empire[73]'. An example of this is the IRA's Kilmichael ambush which is said to have 'jerked the people of India to a new appraisal of their position. Egypt stood amazed. It ultimately pervaded darkest Africa[74]'. According to Bew, Gibbon and Patterson: 'Struggles over the status of the north are no more automatically anti-imperialist than crimes against property are automatically anti-capitalist[75].' While formally correct this proposition does not take into account the imperial context referred to here. After all unionist leader Lord Craigavon claimed 'Ulster' as 'an outpost of Empire[76]'.

The partition of Ireland has, therefore, to be seen in this imperial and colonial context and became a model for British imperialism. Thus, according to Sir Ronald Storrs, the British governor of Jerusalem under the British Mandate and brain behind Lawrence of Arabia, the purpose behind the Balfour Declaration and the partition of Palestine was for the British Empire to set up 'a loyal Jewish Ulster in a sea of potential hostile Arabism[77]'. The project of creating another 'Ulster' was not limited to the Middle-East. When King George V met the Rhodesian self-government delegates in 1921 in London he told them they were 'the Ulster of South Africa[78]'. The same way Irish republicans inspired other colonised people, Ulster Unionists and Loyalists were a major source of inspiration to colonial settlers in Kenya, Rhodesia and South African Natal defending their privileges against the 'natives'. After all, Lord Milner argued that the rationale behind the creation of Northern Ireland was to 'rescue the white settler colony of Ulster from submersion in a sea of inferior Celts[79]'. The creation of Northern Ireland was very much part of the defence of imperial and colonial rule and some academic studies demonstrate how Ulster Protestants still have retained many attitudes in common with those of settlers in other parts of the world[80].

Colonial entropy

Few studies use a colonial framework to understand the recent conflict in Northern Ireland[81]. Yet it is possible to analyse the conflict there since the late 1960s in the context of the 'small' wars that hastened the end of the British colonial Empire – Palestine, Malaya, Kenya, Cyprus and Aden. Even if Northern Ireland is officially part of the United Kingdom and the British government denies the colonial nature of the problem, London has used in the six counties the same counter-insurgency methods used in these wars[82]. It is also interesting to note that when the conflict erupted, its protagonists understood it through the 'Black Power' prism, insurgents being inspired by the Civil Rights Movement and the Black Panthers in the USA, and the British state interpreting the Irish conflict as a sign of racial and social conflicts to come[83]. Also Irish republicans understood their struggle in the context of the wars mentioned above as well as in a more general context of a global struggle against colonialism and imperialism. 'We ask of England that which America gave to Vietnam, France to Algeria and Britain herself to her former colonies of Palestine, Cyprus and Aden. Britain gained in prestige by withdrawing from those countries; she will win universal respect by withdrawing from her first and last colony,' declared chief republican strategist Daithi Ó Conaill in 1973[84]. Mural paintings in republican areas in the North illustrate for instance their affinities with liberation movements elsewhere in the world, and express their solidarity with those who struggle against imperialism and oppression[85]. Republicans identify with the Palestinians, Cuba or the ANC, as many liberation movements find their mirror image in the Irish resistance. In 1992 for example, Nelson Mandela publically expressed his support for the IRA in its struggle against colonialism[86]. In 2018 the chief negotiator and secretary general of the Palestine Liberation Organisation executive committee wrote that: 'The Palestinian and Irish people share a proud and long history of collective struggle against foreign settler-colonialism in our respective attempts to assert sovereignty and gain independence...We believe that Ireland's history provides you with the moral background to set the example in Europe[87].' On the other hand, unionists and Loyalists identify with Israel and the Afrikaners[88]. The left has often seen the struggle of Irish republicans against the British state as being the vanguard of anti-imperialist struggle in Europe. For example, books published in Italy, Germany and France during the 1970s saw Northern Ireland as 'a Vietnam in Europe'.[89] More particularly, some currents of the radical left in Britain saw the Irish conflict as being 'the key to the British revolution', quoting certain representatives of the British ruling class claiming that if they lost in Belfast, they would soon be losing in Brixton or Birmingham[90]. The problem for the British government is that Northern Ireland is not a distant colony of the British Empire but a part of the United Kingdom, and that its problems intensify the crisis of the British state. If a century ago the struggle in Ireland weakened the British Empire in India and Egypt, the political effect of the republican struggle in the later part of the twentieth century has been to reinforce and radicalise progressive struggles elsewhere in the United Kingdom as the miners strike during the 1980s demonstrated[91].

A study published in 1998, the year of the Belfast Agreement, used the interesting expression of 'colonial entropy' to describe Northern Ireland's relation to the United Kingdom:

Britain's continuing involvement in Ireland is best explained as a form of *colonial entropy*. It is caught in a colonial present because of its colonial past. Across centuries of colonial history, Britain had selfish economic and strategic interests in Ireland and was prepared to defend these interests – whatever the majority of the Irish people wanted. This entropy means that the cost-benefit analysis of the situation is increasingly finely balanced for the British state. The costs of remaining in Ireland – military, financial and ideological – are not sufficient to force a formal withdrawal. Neither are the benefits so great that the British state is prepared to make enormous sacrifices in order to stay in Ireland. The British state is unsure of how to withdraw from Ireland in its interests – as it has done from most of its former colonies – but neither can it see how its long-term interests will be served by remaining in Ireland. Put bluntly, Northern Ireland is no longer 'as British as Finchley' as Margaret Thatcher once famously proclaimed, but it remains slightly more British than Hong Kong[92].

A limit of this interesting analysis is that Northern Ireland could be more of what Michael Hechter called an 'internal' colony than an 'external' colony like Hong Kong. The concept of 'internal colonialism' developed by Michael Hechter finds its genesis in Lenin's analysis of the development of capitalism in Russia and Gramsci's study of the 'Southern Question' in Italy and is used by Hechter to describe the relation of the celtic fringe of the United Kingdom to London[93].

Republicanism and the universal

This study is written from the standpoint of Irish republicanism[94]. The public unfortunately has often a wrong idea of its nature, believing it is fundamentally about fanatic Irish Nationalists seeking to reunify Ireland through armed actions. In fact a critical view of nationalism is entirely compatible with it. Leading socialist republican Peadar O'Donnell stated in 1985: 'The world is not composed of nations, it is not a complex of nations. It's full of people! And they have one thing in common, they want to live[95].' Republicanism in Ireland is a product of the philosophical discourse of modernity, more particularly of what has been called the 'radical enlightenment' rather than the romantic nationalist reaction against it:

> The revolutionary ideology that emerged in Ireland in the last quarter of the eighteenth century aimed to establish a democratic, secular and independent Irish republic that would take its place in a New World Order shaped by the forces of Enlightenment and revolution and usher in a new and better era for humanity. It foresaw government and social institutions reshaped according to the interests and desires of the people, and the removal of the burdens placed on them by the demands of kings, aristocrats, and priests. In this new world, liberty would be triumphant, poverty alleviated, and old hatred resolved. This was in accordance with the political ideas associated with the Radical Enlightenment. There were other sources of motivation for revolutionaries in 1790s Ireland, including Milleniarism, radical Lockeanism, classical Republicanism, social and economic grievances, and even in some cases a hope for Catholic 'revanche', but the ideology of the United Irishmen was unmistakebly shaped by the most radical political ideas that sprung from the Enlightenment.[96]

It is a direct expression of the 'Revolution in the Form of

Thought' which took place in Ireland between 1789 and 1798[97]. Wolfe Tone, the founder of republicanism in Ireland, and his movement the United Irishmen sought to supplant a political system rooted in sectarian privilege with a secular democratic politics, founded on universal ideas of equality and justice and this was deliberately blocked by the British state, using the weapons of sectarianism and military terror[98]. There are clear affinities between the United Irishmen Republicans in Ireland and the Black Jacobins of Toussaint Louverture in Haiti – as Kevin Whelan noted, there is clear evidence that many United Irishmen were inspired by the Haitian Revolution, and Louverture's leadership in particular[99]. Republicanism is based on universal principles, unlike nationalism which is based on the particular. Even the Young Ireland movement often associated with cultural nationalism was not a romantic retreat from politics, or simply an aesthetic expression of a desire for national independence: it was an ambitious attempt to recover an ancient ideal of citizenship for a modern democratic age[100]. Culturally speaking, in his 1992 essay 'Identity without a Centre: Allegory, History and Irish Nationalism', Luke Gibbons argues that Irish nationalism figures the self-images of a culture in *allegorical* terms, with all the contestation of identity and openess towards the other which that entails[101]. Allegorical versions of Irish identity, for Gibbons, are a means through which 'nationalism from below' expresses itself and serves as a vehicle for social transformation. Republicanism in Ireland is far more than a 'nationalist' or 'separatist' project. Breaking the connection with the United Kingdom has been the necessary pre-requisite to establising a republic, rather than an end in itself, it is solely a means for social and political progress. This is where its egalitarian dimension comes in. Irish republicanism represents since the beginning the interests of subaltern classes, not those of the ruling classes. In his journal on 11 March 1796, Theobald Wolfe Tone wrote: 'Our independence must be had at all hazards, if the men of property will not support us, they must fall: we can support ourselves by the aid of that numerous and respectable class of the community, the men of no property[102].' This reference to the propertyless, the poor, the common people shows the social basis of Irish republicanism and its plebeian nature. James Fintan Lalor, a major figure of nineteenth-century Irish republicanism, wrote that the aim was not simply to 'Repeal the Union' with Great Britain but to 'Undo the Conquest' by which he understands the social and economic property relations established by the British presence[103]. The great socialist and republican James Connolly warned in 1897: 'If you remove the English army tomorrow and hoist the green flag… unless you set about the organisation of the socialist republic your efforts will be vain…Nationalism without Socialism…is only national recreancy[104].' As to the nature of the republic aimed for, Connolly writes: 'The Republic I would wish our fellow-countrymen to set before them as their ideal should be of such character that the mere mention of its name would at all times serve as a beacon-light to the oppressed of every land, at all times holding forth promise of freedom and plenteousness as the reward of their efforts on its behalf[105].' A look at the 1803, 1867 and 1916 Proclamations of an Irish Republic will provide a good glimpse into the nature of the ideology[106]. The 1867 Proclamation is particularly remarkable. It resists ideas of either religious or ethnic solidarity as the basis for the Irish Republic. It is explicitly secular and does not create a simple opposition of 'Irish' to 'English'. It declares war on 'aristocratic locusts, whether English or Irish, who have eaten the verdure of our fields'. On the other hand it claims a common cause with the English working class: 'As for you, workmen of England, it is not only your hearts we wish, but your arms.' It is thus wrong to understand Irish republicanism as being a simple form of nationalism. Especially as it has a very strong internationalist element. 'We mean to be free, and in every enemy of tyranny we recognise a brother, wherever be his birthplace, in every enemy of freedom we also recognise our enemy, though he were as Irish as our hills,[107] wrote Connolly. Irish republicanism is in solidarity with all those who struggle against imperialism and oppression all over the world. Among the most remarkable examples that this tradition has produced, one can mention Roger Casement who was the first to expose the crimes of King Leopold in the Belgian Congo and the exploitation of natives in Brazil by the multinational companies or the Irish republicans who joined the international brigades to fight fascism in Spain. The intellectual references of Irish republicanism go way beyond Irish shores. A study examining the IRA library in Long Kesh prison shows on top of books on Irish republicanism a huge collection of books ranging from the classics of historical materialism from Marx to Gramsci to the theoricians of revolutionary thirdworldism such as Frantz Fanon, Che Guevara or Amilcar Cabral[108]. One can thus see that Irish republicanism transcends a particular 'nationalist' project for a much more universal one based on justice. If there is one key idea that the reader should remember it is that of liberation and the universal.

Irish republicanism is also misunderstood if presented as being essentially in favour of armed struggle against the British state. First, because this pays more attention to the 'means' rather than the 'ends' which will give a deformed idea of the subject. Second, because in the course of over 2 centuries, Irish republicans have used a huge number of tactics in their struggle which was never limited to armed actions: boycott, electoral interventions, strikes, mass struggles...It is only in exceptional circumstances that armed struggle has been on the agenda. 'We believe in constitutional action in normal times; we believe in revolutionary action in exceptional times,' wrote Connolly[109]. Anti-colonial nationalist movements as Ireland shows 'have been multifaceted, and their social and cultural dimensions rather than their insurrectionary nature may be their most enduring characteristics[110]. Third, because Irish republicanism has been critical of militarist deviations. James Connolly for instance wrote a very famous polemic against what he called 'the physical force party' in Irish politics[111]. It is not well known but there is even a pacifist current within Irish republicanism, whose most famous representative is Francis Sheehy-Skeffington, later murdered by the British Army[112]. But it is important to emphasise the revolutionary nature of Irish republicanism. In 2018 the new Junior Certificate history course in the Republic of Ireland (Irish equivalent of A-levels) states: 'Explore how the physical force tradition impacted on Irish politics, with particular reference to a pre-twentieth century example of a rebellion.' It is interesting how the American revolutionaries of 1776 and the French revolutionaries of 1789 are said to be engaged in 'revolution', whereas the Irish revolutionaries of 1798, 1803, 1848 and 1867 are stated to be a 'physical force tradition' engaged in 'rebellion'. Their legacy is far greater than being considered 'a physical force tradition' engaged in 'rebellion'. Such Irish men and women and their successors deserve the title 'revolutionaries'[113]. As Tommy McKearney put it:

> Throughout the past two centuries, *The Republic* has been a vehicle for certain sections of the Irish people that have felt mistreated, politically impotent and unable to gain redress through conventional parliamentary means. Whether through accident or design, whenever a significant number of the population felt the need to join in the campaign for this goal, *The Republic* acquires a fresh dynamic. In a real sense, *The Republic* is the goal of Irish people in revolt and it becomes a serious possibility if it ever turns out to be the Irish people in revolt.[114]

Étienne Balibar in a 2004 essay entitled 'Palestine: A Universal Cause' links the question of Palestine to democracy and its claims of universality[115]. The plight of the Palestinians is not merely a local matter, a regional dispute, it touches all of us, he argues, to the extent that we are all compelled to imagine and invent the conditions for justice and equality in a post-colonial era[116]. The ambition of this study is to do the same and present the Irish struggle for freedom as symbolic of a more universal human struggle against oppression, injustice and exploitation. It stresses that it is part of something much wider. The liberation project allows us to distinguish Irish republicanism from a particular nationalism, and it is imperative to encourage the development of its universal and emancipatory content. We need 'to respect the truth of the past facts, the urgent necessities of the present and the justice of future perspectives', concluded Balibar. As Slavoj Žižek once said: 'Irishmen, yet another effort, if you want to become republicans![117]'

Conclusion

It is interesting that leading historian Roy Foster, former Carroll Professor of Irish History at Oxford University, noted that the people who study Irish history are no longer drawn mainly from those with Irish backgrounds.

They're people who think that Ireland is an interesting country with a fascinating history that reflects all sorts of enormous issues about colonialism, postcolonialism, violence – all those issues that we're now groping with all over the world – and that Ireland and the study of Irish history can illuminate these in a very interesting and sometimes anticipatory way, particularly at the turn of the last century[118].

The present study totally shares this perspective. The conflict in Northern Ireland is not just some revolt in a distant colony or a simple dispute about a border – it is a challenge to the power and the legitimacy of the British state and its ruling class in Ireland in a global context of struggles against imperialism and colonialism. There is much at stake for the British state in Northern Ireland. In a famous editorial dated 21 November 1979, *The Times* remarked that the conflict in Northern Ireland 'concern(s) the most fundamental of all political issues: allegiance, national identity, the legitimacy of the state'. The strategic imperative of successive British governments has been to contain the Irish challenge to its authority. The peace process has to be seen as an attempt by the British state to reconstruct its authority in Northern Ireland in a context of decline and defeat of actually existing national liberation movements.

Endnotes

1   Michael McHugh, Good Friday Agreement's tenets now used globally, *Belfast Telegraph*, 6 April 2018

2   See: David Miller (1994), *Don't Mention the War: Northern Ireland, Propaganda and the Media*, London: Pluto Press

3   Greg McLaughlin and Stephen Baker (2010), *The Propaganda of Peace: The Role of Media and Culture in the Northern Ireland Peace Process*, Bristol: Intellect

4   Document available: http://cain.ulst.ac.uk/events/peace/docs/nio26398.htm

5   Ed Moloney (2006), The Peace Process and Journalism, in: *Britain & Ireland: Lives Entwined II*, London: The British Council, 65-82

6   Laura Slattery, 'Dissident journalists' find the going tough up North, *Irish Times*, 25 October 2012, Brendan Hughes, Stormont press officers outnumber Scottish and Welsh governments, *Irish News*, 22 September 2016

7   Dan Keenan, Changed North brings media review of operations, *Irish Times*, 21 July 2007

8   Lorna Siggins, Peace in NI bought by 'fraud and lying', says McAliskey, *Irish Times*, 30 April 2007

9   Paul Dixon, The truth about the Good Friday Agreement is

that, if it wasn't for deliberate deceptions, there would be no peace process here, *Belfast Telegraph*, 28 March 2018

10　Tony Blair 'lied to stop Northern Ireland peace talks collapsing', *Daily Telegraph*, 1 September 2010

11　Interview with Brendan Hughes, *Fourthwrite*, Issue 1, Spring 2000

12　Paul Dixon (2002), Political Skills or Lying and Manipulation? The Choregraphy of the Northern Ireland Peace Process, *Political Studies*, 50:4, 725-741. See also Arthur Aughey (2002), The Art and Effect of Political Lying in Northern Ireland, *Irish Political Studies*, 17:2,1-16

13　David Mitchell (2009), Cooking the Fudge: Constructive Ambiguity and the Implementation of the Northern Ireland Agreement, 1998-2007, *Irish Political Studies*, 24:3, 321-336

14　Jim Gibney, Ambiguity: Oiling wheels of progress, *An Phoblacht-Republican News*, 17 April 2003

15　Noam Chomsky (1997), *World Orders: Old and New*, London: Pluto Press, 238-239, 274

16　Roy Foster, Partnership of Loss, *London Review of Books*, 13 December 2007

17　Liz Curtis (1994), *The Cause of Ireland: From the United Irishmen to Partition*, Belfast: Beyond the Pale, 284

18　Parl Deb, 5 (Lords), 14 December 1921, Volume 48 col 44

19　Hansard, Volume 127, Column 1322

20　For example: Six-County Exclusion Plan: Irish Unionists Voice Their Opposition, *Newsletter*, 22 June 1916

21　Hansard, 18 June 1912, Volume 39, cols. 1076

22　House of Common debates, 5th series, volume 123, col.1198, 22 December 1919

23　Hansard, 18 June 1912, Volume 39, cols 1121-1124

24　Hansard, 18 June 1912, Volume 39, cols 1074-1075

25　The Murray family from Gortineddan whose house was split in the middle between counties Fermanagh in Northern Ireland and Cavan in the South famously illustrates this point. Cfr. Peter Leary (2016), *Unapproved Routes: Histories of the Irish Border, 1922-1972*, Oxford University Press, 116-117

26 Michael O'Regan, Brexit negotiator says EU will not allow Ireland to suffer, *Irish Times*, 21 September 2017. See also: Freya McClements, David Crockett and the Border farm split by the wild frontier, *Irish Times*, 31 October 2017

27 M.J. MacManus (1947), *Eamon de Valera: A Biography*, Dublin: Talbot Press, 328

28 *Irish Times* 30 July 1912. On this issue see also: James Anderson (1980), Regions and Religions in Ireland: A Short Critique of the 'Two Nations' Theory, *Antipode*, 12:1, 44-53

29 Hansard. 11 June 1912, Volume 34, col 787

30 Hansard, Volume 46, col 476

31 Hansard, 30 April 1912, Volume 37, cols 1720-1721

32 Hansard, 9 March 1914, vol xlix, col 938

33 John Whyte (1990), *Interpreting Northern Ireland*, Oxford University Press, 163-164

34 Paul Bew, Peter Gibbon, Henry Patterson (1979), *The State in Northern Ireland*, Manchester: Manchester University Press, 221

35 Richard English (1998), *Ernie O'Malley: IRA Intellectual*, Oxford: Oxford University Press, 173 - emphasis in the original. See also: Clare O'Halloran (1987), *Partition and the Limits of Irish Nationalism: An Ideology Under Stress*, Dublin: Gill and Macmillan, 17-18

36 Joe Cleary (2002), *Literature, Partition and the Nation State: Culture and Conflict in Ireland, Israel and Palestine*, Cambridge: Cambridge University Press, 34 - emphasis in the original

37 The Sunday Times Insight Team (1972), *Ulster*, Harmondsworth: Penguin Books, 306-307

38 Michael Farrell, *Northern Ireland: The Orange State*, London: Pluto Press, 1976, 93-94, 97

39 Paul Bew, Peter Gibbon, Henry Patterson (1979), op.cit., 70
40 Anthony Jennings (ed) (1988), *Justice Under Fire: The Abuse of Civil Liberties in Northern Ireland*, London: Pluto Press
41 Patrick J. McGrory L.L.B. (1986), *Emergency Legislation - Law and the Constitution: Present Discontents*, Derry: Field Day Pamphlet Number 12, 27-28
42 Chris Gilligan (2002), Devolving Power? Human Rights and State Regulation in Northern Ireland, in David Chandler (ed), *Rethinking Human Rights Critical Approaches to International Politics*, Basingstoke: Palgrave Macmillan, 79-80
43 As demontrated by a detailed study of people directly killed by the state: Fionnuala Ní Aolaín (2000), *The Politics of Force: Conflict Management and State Violence in Northern Ireland*, Belfast: The Blackstaff Press
44 Giorgio Agamben (2003), *État d'Exception. Homo Sacer II:1*, Paris: Editions du Seuil, chapter 1. See: Claire Delisle (2012), *Leading to Peace: Prisoner Resistance and Leadership Development in the IRA and Sinn Fein*, PhD thesis, Department of Criminology, University of Ottawa, 116-131 for the application of Agamben's theories in the case of Northern Ireland and republicans as *Homo Sacer*
45 Robbie McVeigh (1998), The British/Irish 'Peace Process' and the Colonial Legacy, in James Anderson and James Goodman (eds), *Dis/Agreeing Ireland: Contexts, Obstacles, Hopes*, London: Pluto Press, 40
46 Sydney Elliott and W.D. Flackes (1999), *Northern Ireland: A Political Directory 1968-1999*, Belfast, The Blackstaff Press, fifth revised and updated edition, 681-687
47 Brendan O'Leary and John McGarry (1996), *The Politics of Antagonism: Understanding Northern Ireland*, London: The Athlone Press, Second Edition, 12-13, 18
48 Karola Dillenburger, Response, in B. Hamber, D. Kulle, R. Wilson (eds), *Future Policies for the Past*, Belfast: Democratic

Dialogue Report No.13, February 2001

49   Brendan O'Leary and John McGarry (1996), op.cit., 34

50   Bob Rowthorn and Naomi Wayne (1988), *Northern Ireland: the Political Economy of Conflict*, Cambridge: Polity Press, 6-7

51   Figures from: Bill Rolston (2000), *Unfinished Business: State Killings and the Quest for Truth*, Belfast: Beyond The Pale

52   Roy Greenslade, A Hierarchy of Death, *The Guardian*, 19 April 2007

53   Marie-Louise McCrory, More than 250 children killed during Troubles, *The Irish News*, 16 August 2010

54   Peter R. Neumann (2009), *Old and New Terrorism: Late Modernity, Globalization and the Transformation of Political Violence*, Cambridge: Polity Press, 6-7

55   Brendan O'Leary and John McGarry (1996), op.cit., 268-269

56   T.K. Wilson (2010), *Frontiers of Violence: Conflict and Identity in Ulster and Upper Silesia, 1918-1922*, Oxford: Oxford University Press, for an interesting analysis

57   Edward W. Said (1994), *The Pen and the Sword: Conversations with David Barsamian*, Edinburgh: AK Press, 65

58   Edward W. Said (1993), *Culture and Imperialism*, London: Chatto & Windus, 284

59   Stephen Howe (2000), *Ireland and Empire: Colonial Legacies in Irish History and Culture*, Oxford University Press, for the most erudite polemic against 'anti-colonial' analyses. See also: Stephen Howe (2008), Questioning the (bad) question: 'Was Ireland a colony?', *Irish Historical Studies*, 36: 142, 138-152. Interestingly, by 2009 Howe could write: 'Sometimes it is a pleasure to have one's claims refuted and one's previous intellectual positions reversed, or at least rapidly outdated.' Since the publication in 2000 of his highly critical analysis, 'a rapidly growing literature has almost overturned the judgement, exploring numerous aspects of these relationships with unprecedented, ever-

growing care, detail and attention to complexity and nuance'. Stephen Howe (2009), 'Minding the Gaps: New Directions in the Study of Ireland and Empire', *Journal of Imperial and Commonwealth History*, 37:1, 136

60 Joe Cleary (2007), Amongst Empires: A Short History of Ireland and Empire Studies in International Context, *Eire-Ireland*, 42:1-2, 11-57 for an overview

61 For a very useful overview see: Terrence McDonough (ed) (2005), *Was Ireland a Colony? Economy, Politics, Ideology and Culture in Nineteenth-Century Ireland*, Dublin: Irish Academic Press

62 Richard Hill (2015), Policing Ireland, Policing Colonies: The Irish Constabulary 'Model', in: Angela McCarthy (ed), *Ireland in the World: Comparative, Transnational,and Personal Perspectives*, London: Routledge, 61-81

63 Paul A. Townend (2016), *The Road to Home Rule: Anti-Imperialism and the Irish National Movement*, Madison: University of Wisconsin Press

64 Maurice Walsh (2015), *Bitter Freedom: Ireland in a Revolutionary World 1918-23*, London: Faber & Faber, 132-133 on Ho Chi Minh for example

65 For an overall view see: Kate O'Malley (2006), Ireland, India and Empire: Indo-Irish separatist political links and perceived threats to the British Empire, in: Tadhg Foley and Maureen O'Connor (eds), *Ireland and India: Colonies, Culture and Empire*, Dublin: Irish Academic Press, 225-232; and also Kate O'Malley (2008), *Ireland, India and Empire: Indo-Irish Radical Connections 1919-1964*, Manchester: Manchester University Press

66 Jason Knirck (2017), The Irish Revolution and World History: Nation, Race, and Civilization in the Rhetoric of the Irish Revolutionary Generation, *Éire-Ireland*, 52: 3 and 4, 173-174

67 See: Irish Anti-Colonial Struggle and Black Radical Politics

in: Cathy Bergin (ed) (2016), *African American Anti-Colonial Thought 1917-1937*, Edinburgh: Edinburgh University Press, 58-82; also the chapter 'Negro Sinn Féiners and Black Fenians: 'Heroic Ireland' and the Black Nationalist Imagination' in Bruce Nelson (2012), *Irish Nationalists and the Making of the Irish Race*, NJ: Princeton University Press, 181-211

68 Jean-Paul Sartre, Préface à Frantz Fanon (1961), *Les Damnés de la Terre*, Paris: François Maspero, 9

69 Quoted in: Deirdre McMahon (1999), Ireland and the Empire-Commonwealth 1900-1948, in Judith Brown and William Roger Lewis (eds), *The Oxford History of the British Empire. Volume IV: The Twentieth Century*, Oxford: Oxford University Press, 146

70 Parl Deb, 5 (Lords), 14 December 1921, vol.48 Col.41

71 Thomas Jones (1971), *Whitehall Diary Volume III. Ireland 1918-1925*, London: Oxford University Press, 109

72 *Lenin on Ireland* (1970), Dublin: New Books, 33-34

73 Quoted in: Donal Lowry (1996), Ulster Resistance and the Loyalist Rebellion in the Empire, in: Keith Jeffery (ed), *'An Irish Empire'? Aspects of Ireland and the British Empire*, Manchester: Manchester University Press, 197

74 Peter Hart (1998), *The IRA and its Enemies: Violence and Community in Cork 1916-1923*, Oxford University Press, 22

75 Paul Bew, Peter Gibbon, Henry Patterson (1979), op.cit., 29

76 From a quote in Clare O'Halloran (1987), op.cit., 8

77 Cfr. Moshé Machover (2012), *Israelis and Palestinians: Conflict and Resolution*, Chicago: Haymarket Books, 185 and 270; see also: Tom Segev (1999), *One Palestine, Complete: Jews and Arabs under the British Mandate*, New York: Henry Holt, 91. The best comparison between Ireland and Palestine can be found in: Joe Cleary (2002), *Literature, Partition and the Nation State: Culture and Conflict in Ireland, Israel and Palestine*, Cambridge University Press. See in particular

chapter 1: Ireland, Palestine and the antinomies of self-determination in 'the badlands of modernity', 15-50

78 Quoted in: Donal Lowry (1996), op.cit., 196

79 Quoted in: Fergal McCluskey (2014), *The Irish Revolution: Tyrone 1912-23*, Dublin: Four Courts Press, 134

80 See in particular: Pamela Clayton (1996), Enemies and Passing Friends: Settler Ideologies in Twentieth Century Ulster, London: Pluto Press

81 David Miller (1998), Colonialism and Academic Representations of the Troubles, in David Miller (ed), *Rethinking Northern Ireland: Culture, Ideology and Colonialism*, Harlow: Longman, 3-39 for a defence of the colonial paradigm

82 John Newsinger (2002), *British Counterinsurgency: From Palestine to Northern Ireland*, Basingstoke: Palgrave

83 Simon Prince (2015), 'Do What The Afro-Americans Are Doing': Black Power and the start of the Northern Ireland Troubles, *Journal of Contemporary History*, 50:3, 516-535

84 Quoted on the back cover of: Provisional IRA (1973), *Freedom Struggle*, no publisher

85 Bill Rolston (2009), 'The Brothers on the Wall': International Solidarity and Irish Political Murals, *Journal of Black Studies*, 39:3, 446-470

86 Mandela tells of support for IRA on TV, *Irish Times*, 19 October 1992

87 Dr Saeb Erekat, Ireland must not support Israeli settlement project, *Irish Times*, 24 February 2018

88 Donal Lowry (1996), op.cit., 205-208 and Marie-Violaine Louvet (2016), *Civil Society, Post-Colonialism and Transnational Solidarity: The Irish and the Middle East Conflict*, London: Palgrave Macmillan, 197-217 for loyalists and Israel and 95 -164 for republicans and the Palestinians

89 Lotta Continua (1972), *Irlanda: Un Vietnam in Europa*, Milano: Edizioni di Lotta Continua; Trikont Verlag (1972),

Irland, ein Vietnam in Europa, München: Schriften zum Klassenkampf Nr. 32; Roger Faligot (1977), *La Résistance Irlandaise,* Paris: François Maspero, 9. Also: The Men of No Property (1975), *England's Vietnam: Irish Songs of Resistance,* Resistance Records RES 1001 LP

90   David Reed (1984), *Ireland: The Key to the British Revolution,* London: Larkin Publications, 384

91   David Reed and Olivia Adamson (1985) *Miners Strike, 1984-1985: People Versus State,* London: Larkin Publications, 66 and for reactions from prisoners in the H-Blocks see 117-121

92   Robbie McVeigh (1998), The British/Irish 'Peace Process' and the Colonial Legacy, op.cit., 35

93   Michael Hechter (1975), *Internal Colonialism: The Celtic Fringe in British National Development, 1536-1966,* London: Routledge and Kegan Paul, 8-9

94   More generally the author is totally in line with: Jan Selby (2006), Edward W. Said: Truth, Justice and Nationalism, *interventions,* 8:1, 40-55. For an excellent defence of nationalism in an emancipatory context see in particlar: Pheng Cheah (2003) *Spectral Nationality: Passages of Freedom from Kant to Postcolonial Literatures of Liberation,* New York: Columbia University Press and in the particular case of Ireland Terry Eagleton (1999), Nationalism and the Case of Ireland, *New Left Review,* Issue 234, 44-61

95   Peadar O'Donnell (1986), *Monkeys in the Superstructure: Reminiscences of Peadar O'Donnell,* Galway: Salmon Publishing, 29

96   Ultán Gillen (2017), Radical Enlightenment and Revolution in Late Eighteenth-Century Ireland, in Steffen Ducheyne (ed) *Reassessing the Radical Enlightenment,* London: Routledge, 240-257

97   Thomas Metscher (1989), Between 1789 and 1798: the 'Revolution in the Form of Thought' in Ireland, *Études*

irlandaises, 14:1, 139-146

98 Kevin Whelan (1996), *The Tree of Liberty: Radicalism, Catholicism and the Construction of Irish Identity 1760-1830*, Indiana: University of Notre Dame Press, 99-130

99 Charles Forsdick and Christian Høgsbjerg (2017), *Toussaint Louverture: A Black Jacobin in the Age of Revolutions*, London: Pluto Press, 132

100 David Dwan (2008), *The Great Community: Culture and Nationalism in Ireland*, Dublin: Field Day, 23-75

101 Luke Gibbons (1996) *Transformations in Irish Culture*, Cork University Press in association with Field Day, 134-149. It is beyond the scope of this study to show how allegory prevents republicanism from colluding with an 'aesthetic ideology' in contrast to nationalism which is tied to symbol rather than allegory

102 Jim Smyth (1992), *The Men of No Property: Irish Radicals and Popular Politics in the Late Eighteenth Century*, London: Macmillan, ix-x

103 Quoted in: Gerry Kearns (2014), 'Up to the Sun and Down to the Centre': The Utopian Moment in Anticolonial Nationalism, *Historical Geography*, 42, 145

104 James Connolly (1987), *Collected Works: 1*, Dublin: New Books, 307

105 In the same place, 305

106 John O'Neill, Proclamations of an Irish Republic, 1803, 1867, 1916, Treason Felony Blog, 31 March 2016; Proclamation of 1803, 1867 and 1916, by Padraig Óg Ó Ruairc https://www.youtube.com/watch?v=AX9I9bJJ_IM

107 James Connolly (1987), op.cit., 314. In a letter to Karl Kautsky dated 7 February 1882 Friedrich Engels noted that the Irish 'have not only the right but even the duty to be nationalistic before they become internationalistic'. (Karl Marx and Friedrich Engels (1971), *Ireland and the Irish Question*, Moscow: Progress Publishers, 449-450)

108 Richard English (2003), *Armed Struggle: A History of the IRA*, London: Macmillan, 232-237

109 James Connolly (1988), op.cit., 117

110 Shakir Mustafa (1998), Revisionism and Revival: A Postcolonial Approach to Irish Cultural Nationalism, *New Hibernia Review*, 2:3, 36

111 James Connolly (1987), op.cit., 335-339

112 Leah Levenson (1983), *With wooden sword: a portrait of Francis Sheehy-Skeffington, militant pacifist*, Boston: Northeastern University Press

113 https://www.irishexaminer.com/breakingnews/views/ yourview/readers-blog-irish-battle-for-freedom-was-a- true-revolution-834412.html

114 Tommy McKearney, Wither the Republic?, *Fortnight*, Issue 392, February 2001, 18-19

115 Étienne Balibar, Universalité de la cause palestinienne, *Le Monde Diplomatique*, Mai 2004

116 See also the remarkable essay by Tom Paulin (2005), Cultural Struggle and Memory: Palestine-Israel, South Africa and Northern Ireland in Historical Perspective, *Holy Land Studies*, 4:1, 5-16

117 Slavoj Žižek (1993), From Courtly Love to The Crying Game, *New Left Review*, Issue 202, 107

118 Roy Foster: 'The Irish argue about history all the time', *Irish Times*, 1 October 2016

Part Two. The 'Process': one step forward or two steps backwards?

Good Friday: the death of Irish Republicanism
Anthony McIntyre (2008)

The life of the spirit is not the life that shrinks from death and keeps itself untouched by devastation, but rather the life that endures the presence of death within itself and preserves itself alive within death. It wins its truth only when, in utter dismemberment, it finds itself...Spirit is this power only by looking the negative in the face, and tarrying with it. This tarrying with the negative is magical power that converts it into being.
G.W.F Hegel (1807), Preface to The Phenomenology of Spirit

Self-determination as foundation of a lasting peace

The right to self-determination occupies a central place in Irish republican thinking[1] – without self-determination, no liberation is possible. It is thus not surprising that feminist arguments made by Irish republican activists have been based upon the right of self-determination of women over their own sexuality[2]. The right of self-determination has been used as an instrument of liberation – for instance by colonised people for their national emancipation. The right of self-determination is used here in this context, and not as the one used for example in the case of secessionist demands in Singapore (1965) or Bangladesh (1971), nor that of German reunification (1990) or the independence of Kosovo (2008). More broadly, the right of people to self-determination is a cardinal principle of modern international law, incorporated into the UN charter. It is not a new idea. In 1918, Woodrow Wilson, the US president whose '14 points' speech set out principles for world peace, declared: 'National aspirations must be respected; people may now be dominated

45

and governed only by their own consent. 'Self-determination' is not a mere phrase; it is an imperative principle of action.' It certainly has been 'an imperative principle of action' and not a 'mere phrase' for Irish republicans from the very moment Wilson raised the issue[3].

In the light of the prevailing interpretation of the principle of self-determination it is the right of the majority to establish an independent state within any area administered as a political entity by a colonial power. Britain has maintained some presence on the island of Ireland for over 800 years, and debate of whether contemporary circumstances in the north of Ireland constitute a form of colonialism has been almost entirely stifled as seen earlier; not to mention that the extent to which Ireland has been 'conquered' in terms of international law remains highly controversial[4]. For republicans, however, Northern Ireland was an artificially created entity; its genesis was illegitimate not merely because it partitioned the island but because of the particular boundaries drawn. Consequently Northern Ireland's inclusion within the United Kingdom constitutes a denial of the right to self-determination of the majority within the island. Seán MacBride (1904-1988) has to date been the most prominent and respected Irish republican able to articulate and defend this analysis at an international level. He rose from being a Chief of Staff of the IRA to an Irish government minister, and subsequently a prominent international politician. He was Ireland's Foreign Minister from 1948 to 1951 and an Assistant Secretary General of the United Nations and United Nations Commissioner for Namibia. He was Secretary General of the International Commission of Jurists and remained a member of that rights group until his death. He was a founder of Amnesty International in 1961 and served as its chairman until 1975. He received the Nobel Peace Prize in 1974, the Lenin Peace Prize for 1975-1976 and the UNESCO Silver Medal. This analysis is thus not just confined to insignificant elements.

The international community has recognised the validity of the self-determination claims of peoples in Namibia, East Timor and Palestine; however a number of obstacles have prevented this from applying in the case of Northern Ireland. First, owing to Britain's international standing as a military and political power, the British state has largely succeeded in convincing the international community that it is a domestic problem internal to the United Kingdom requiring no external interference. Second, the Dublin government, seeking to contain the problem north of its border, has not raised the issue in the United Nations since 1969. Third, the international law on self-determination has itself been insufficiently decolonised as recent studies have shown in the case of indigenous peoples in Australia and Irish Nationalists in the north of Ireland. For varying reasons, these claimants do not pass the 'salt-water' colonial test, and their claims have not adequately been addressed by the international community. Instead, claimant groups are abandoned to the political whims of their administering states. A 'counter-hegemonic' reading of what international law understands as 'colonialism' and 'self-determination' is required in these two cases, which demonstrates that in the twenty-first century decolonisation remains an unfinished project[5].

What is the significance of the right to self-determination in the context of the peace process? The right of the people of Ireland to self-determination as a whole is what allows 'peace' to go hand in hand with 'justice'. It is simultaneously the best means which enables us to rectify the historic injustice of partition and the best means of ensuring long-term peace and security. This is why it is of crucial importance. If the process is not built on the recognition of the right to self-determination, one can question the 'just' and 'lasting' nature of the peace it is supposed to bring. It is to establish whether it enables peace with justice that this chapter will pay particular attention to the concept of 'self-determination' as it has been used during the process.

Lines of political demarcation

The first time the IRA entered into negotiations with the British government during the 1968-1998 conflict was on 7 July 1972, when an IRA delegation – including Gerry Adams and Martin McGuinness who later became key participants in the negotiations leading to the 1998 Agreement – was flown over to London for discussions with the British government. The three central political demands of Irish Republicans – Sinn Féin and the IRA – were:

1. A British declaration of intent to withdraw from Northern Ireland within 5 years.
2. An all-Ireland constituent Assembly to democratically determine the future of the island.
3. The release of all persons imprisoned as a result of the conflict[6].

But the British state's alternative to the political demands of Irish republicanism in 1972/1973 was already the following:

1. British sovereignty over Northern Ireland remains intact and no change of this without the consent of a majority in the six counties.
2. A local assembly in Northern Ireland in which nationalists and unionists share power.
3. Cross-border bodies between the two parts of the island to recognise the 'Irish dimension'[7].

Democracy is the central concept of republicanism. It holds that the people of Ireland have a right to self-determination as a unit without external impediment – all-Ireland democracy. It rejects the British state's interference in Irish affairs as a barrier to democracy and views this as the root cause of the conflict in Ireland. A declaration by the British government of its intent to withdraw from Ireland is thus a necessary pre-requisite to a solution to the conflict. But for Downing Street, as government of the United Kingdom of Great Britain and Northern Ireland, the Union is self-evident. The conflict is seen as internal to Northern Ireland – two divided communities – and the solution is a local assembly in which the two communities will share power. From a republican point of view, the recognition of the right to self-determination of the people of Ireland as a unit is crucial. But for the British state while this demand is perfectly valid as an aspiration, it refuses to acknowledge it as a right. It is only prepared to concede cross-border bodies to recognise the 'Irish dimension'.

For the British state there can be no changes in the constitutional position of Northern Ireland without the consent of a majority there. This is a key aspect of British policy[8]. But for republicanism to argue that partition is democratic because a majority in the six counties favours it ignores the fact that it is an artificial majority that was created by partition in the first place. Republicanism does not disregard the issue of unionist consent to political arrangements, where it differs from the British state and others is that it refuses unionist consent to be a pre-requisite for constitutional change. While arguing that it is undesirable to coerce a 'minority', republicanism contends that to give a guarantee to a 'minority' in advance against all coercion is to put a premium on unreasonableness and to make a settlement impossible. It will have no incentives to consider other political options so long as the British government gives it unconditional guarantees. The consent of a minority becomes transformed into a veto over the majority – unity by consent of a minority, partition by coercion of the majority[9].

Given such opposite political parameters for resolving the conflict, it is not surprising that earlier peace talks between the IRA and the British government – in 1972 and later in 1975 – led to nothing. If after 20 years of conflict, discussions between Irish republicans and the British government led to the peace process at the beginning of the 1990s, it is because the IRA and Sinn Féin now accepted as the way forward what had been the British state's alternative to republicanism since 1972.

Negotiations: parameters and preconditions

On 1 November 1993, Prime Minister John Major told Westminster that if 'we should sit down and talk with Mr Adams and the Provisional IRA, I can only say that that would turn my stomach...we will not do it'[10]. However, on 28 November 1993, *The Observer* revealed to the public that such dialogue between the British government and the Provisional leadership had been happening for some time[11]. These secret talks would culminate with the IRA declaring a unilateral ceasefire on 31 August 1994 in order to allow Sinn Féin to participate in the peace negotiations which ultimately led to the 1998 Agreement. This, as well as other positive signals from the British and Irish governments, led the Provisional leadership to believe that at some point in the 1990s the London government agreed that the old policy of excluding republicans was futile and that the only strategic alternative was one of inclusion in dialogue and negotiations. However, what goes unmentioned here is that 'the strategic objective was to include republicans while excluding republicanism'[12]. The price to be paid for the inclusion of republicans in the talks was the exclusion of republicanism. This means dialogue with republican leaders and organisations but on the basis of an agenda that excludes the political objectives of republicanism. The whole peace process may have included republicans, but from the 1993 Downing Street Declaration to the final 1998 Belfast Agreement, was always based on the British state's political alternative to republicanism since 1972: an internal solution (a power-sharing assembly in the North which includes nationalists) with the externality of an Irish dimension (cross-border bodies) grafted onto it. The longstanding republican demands were never serious runners for all-party talks, and none of them appeared in the final Belfast Agreement. 'What the British were allowing republicans - by permitting them into all-party talks where they can argue for a united Ireland without the remotest possibility of securing it - is an opportunity to dig a tunnel to the moon[13].'

From a British state perspective 'talking to terrorists' only made sense in the context where the Provisional movement was sufficiently weakened to consider a way out of its campaign as opposed to a general attempt to bring 'extremists' into the 'democratic' process without rigid preconditions. By negotiating with the Provisional movement, the British state was signalling to the IRA a way out of its armed campaign rather than a way out of Ireland for itself. This is evident from the political parameters of the peace process. As Lord David Trimble – the leader of the Ulster Unionist Party during the peace process – later wrote:

> Crucially it was soon made clear (to Republicans) that there were conditions before there could be an official engagement. The key conditions were later formalised in the Downing Street Declaration of 1993 as an end to violence and a commitment to exclusively peaceful and democratic means. Equally important was the government's commitment to the consent principle and its refusal to act as a persuader for a united Ireland, which prefigured the outcome of the formal interparty talks, the three-stranded structure of which were defined in March 1991, and the key procedural decisions taken by the parties in 1992 in the absence of Sinn Féin. When it called the cessation of its campaign in 1994, republicans were, in effect, accepting these parameters for talks.[14]

Examining these parameters and preconditions will confirm this.

The 1993 Downing Street Declaration
The 15 December 1993 *Downing Street Declaration* laid the

parameters for future negotiations. In it, the London and Dublin governments recognised that a political settlement 'may as of right, take the form of agreed structures for the island as a whole, including a united Ireland achieved by peaceful means'. Article 4 of the Declaration stated: 'The British government agree that it is for the people of the island of Ireland alone, by agreement between the two parts respectively, to exercise their right of self-determination on the basis of consent, freely and concurrently given, North and South, to bring about a united Ireland, if that is their wish.' But the 'right' of self-determination was heavily qualified by the fact that constitutional change would be dependent upon the consent of a majority in the North. In Article 2 of the Declaration, the London and Dublin governments committed themselves to Northern Ireland's constitutional guarantee. This implied continued British jurisdiction over Northern Ireland and full recognition of that jurisdiction by the Dublin government. Article 5 had the *Taoiseach* (Irish Prime Minister) on behalf of the Dublin government accepting that 'the democratic right of self-determination by the people of Ireland as a whole must be achieved and exercised with and subject to the agreement and consent of the people of Northern Ireland'. The formula of the Downing Street Declaration ensured that any agreed settlement would be partitionist and copper-fasten the unionist veto. The Downing Street Declaration was bereft of the idea that the British government should 'persuade' the unionists of a united Ireland. In the House of Commons, British Prime Minister John Major stated that the Declaration 'reaffirms the constitutional guarantee in the clearest possible terms':

What is not in the Declaration is any suggestion that the British government should join the ranks of the persuaders of the 'value' and 'legitimacy' of a united Ireland; that is not there. Nor is there any suggestion that the future status of Northern Ireland should be decided by a single act of self-determination by the people of Ireland as a whole; that is not there either. Nor is there any timetable for constitutional change, or any arrangement for joint authority over Northern Ireland. In sum, the Declaration provides that it is, as it must be, for the people of Northern Ireland to determine their own future.[15]

There was a clear political tension between republicanism and the Declaration. As BBC journalist Peter Taylor reminds us, 'Although on the face of it the Joint Declaration was a nationalist green in colour, it was essentially a unionist document effectively enshrining the unionist veto that the Provisionals had spent years fighting to destroy.[16'] While a Sinn Féin conference had rejected the Downing Street Declaration on 24 July 1994, and the IRA statement announcing the ceasefire on 31 August 1994 said it 'is not a solution', subsequent history proves that they had no other options but to accept its parameters. This clearly indicated a shift away from the traditional republican position.

The 1995 Framework Documents

On 22 February 1995 the London and Dublin governments published the *Framework For The Future* documents which provided a possible outline for a political deal. The *Framework For Accountable Government In Northern Ireland* proposed that Northern Ireland should have its own elected assembly with devolved powers. *A New Framework For Agreement* dealt with North-South relations. It envisaged the establishment of cross-border bodies which would seek to harmonise tourism, education and economic development all accountable to the devolved Assembly. As paragraph 10 made clear, the Framework Documents were predicated on the continuation of the Union and that any movement away from that could only be achieved with the agreement of a Northern Ireland Assembly. Paragraph 35 emphasised that North-South bodies would have a role subordinate to the Assembly. Paragraph 21 also stated that the Dublin government would change its constitution to 'reflect the principle of consent'. British Prime Minister John Major reassured unionists that there was a 'triple lock' against constitutional change:

> There is a triple safeguard against any proposals being imposed on Northern Ireland; first, any proposals must command the support of the political parties in Northern Ireland; second, any proposals must then be approved by the people of Northern Ireland in a referendum; and thirdly, any necessary legislation must be passed by this parliament. That provides a triple lock designed to ensure that nothing is implemented without consent.[17]

Despite this the response of the Provisional Republican leadership to the Framework Documents was positive. However, by early 1998, the unionists had succeeded in severely diluting, in the final *Heads of Agreement* documents that had been published by the London and Dublin governments to outline the basis of a settlement on 12 January 1998, most of the cross-border elements that had originally figured in the 1995 Framework Documents, making the Heads of Agreement far less of a threat to unionism than the 1995 Documents[18].

The 1996 Mitchell Principles

On 24 January 1996, the report of the International Body on Arms Decommissioning (also known as the Mitchell Report) published its six principles which sought to establish the entry requirements to political negotiations and define the nature of all future political activity. The principles included renouncing the use of force and a commitment to exclusively peaceful means to resolve political issues, as well as the total disarmament of so-called paramilitary organisations verifiable to the satisfaction of an independent commission. On 9 September 1997, the Sinn Féin leadership signed up to the Mitchell Principles. This was in contradiction with the IRA's constitution as it challenged the IRA's right to bear arms. In accepting the principles, they accepted the British state's definition of what constituted democracy and what it regarded as legitimate opposition. Decommissioning only targeted organisations regarded by the state as illegitimate, while these had to renounce 'violence' the report did not question the state's right to use force. Decommissioning was not synonymous with multilateral demilitarisation. One myth is that the British government and the Unionists were acting in 'bad faith' and created in 1995 the decommissioning issue as a pre-condition to prevent Sinn Féin from taking part in negotiations. For example, in an interview on 14 July 1995 Gerry Adams stated that the decommissioning of IRA weapons had never been mentioned prior to the cessation and that the British government had been aware that a cessation would have been unacceptable to the organisation if decommissioning had been a pre-condition to taking part in negotiations. However, decommissioning had been on the agenda as early as 1993 and had actually been raised by Gerry Adams in an interview on 8 January 1994, almost 9 months prior to the cessation[19].

Republicanising the process or de-republicanising Sinn Féin?

By the time Sinn Féin entered political negotiations on 15 September 1997, the political parameters had been set and on the basis of the Downing Street Declaration, the Framework Documents and the Mitchell Principles any future political arrangement would be a predominantly internal one. The republican political agenda was degraded to the point where Gerry Adams now wrote about 'renegotiating the Union' rather than ending it[20]. The process that the Provisional Republican Movement joined was pre-programmed to deliver a partitionist settlement. At their first ever Downing Street meeting on 11 December 1997, British Prime Minister Tony Blair asked Gerry Adams if he could go back and tell his people 'there was no possibility of a united Ireland'. And at its conclusion Blair told key aides 'he was pleased that Adams seemed to accept he would have to live with something less than a united Ireland' as the outcome of the peace process[21]. In his 2008 book on the process, *Great Hatred Little Room*, former Downing Street chief of staff Jonathan Powell confirms Blair's essentially pro-Union position from the outset of the negotiations leading to the Belfast Agreement. While still leader of the opposition at Westminster, Blair had abandoned Labour's traditional policy of Irish unity by consent. Over time he then moved from a position of ostensible neutrality on the constitutional issue to one of effective support for maintaining the Union of Great Britain and Northern Ireland based on the 'consent' principle subsequently enshrined in the 1998 Belfast Agreement. In a speech given in Belfast in 1997, Prime Minister Blair articulated his position on Northern Ireland in forthright terms:

> My message is simple. I am committed to Northern Ireland. I am committed to the principle of consent...My agenda is not a united Ireland...I believe in the United Kingdom. I value the Union...Northern Ireland will remain part of the United Kingdom as long as a majority here wish...This principle of consent is and will be at the heart of my government's policies on Northern Ireland. It is the key principle...A political settlement is not a slippery slope to a united Ireland. The government will not be persuaders for unity.[22]

The whole parameters and preconditions prevented the Provisionals from 'republicanising' the peace process, in fact the process amounted to a means of 'de-republicanising' Sinn Féin[23]. The process that the Provisional Republican Movement joined was pre-programmed to deliver a partitionist settlement.

Belfast Agreement

The culmination of the peace process was the signing of the Belfast Agreement on (Good Friday) 10 April 1998 after 5pm and its subsequent endorsement in two referenda on 22 May 1998. Not only had the Provisional movement accepted that the talks would not create a united Ireland, but they contributed little to the actual negotiations leading to the 1998 Belfast Agreement, which were essentially driven by the SDLP and the Ulster Unionists[24]. It was no surprise that on 10 December 1998 it was John Hume of the SDLP and David Trimble of the UUP who were jointly awarded the Nobel Peace Prize for their efforts to secure the Belfast Agreement. 'Sinn Féin contributed but little to the political details – "in the dunces corner" as one Irish official put it. But with great tactical brilliance, Adams moved rapidly to embrace the Agreement and claim ownership of it against those who had actually made it.[25]' It was at the margins rather than at the centre that the Provisional movement contributed to the negotiations, mainly on the issue of prisoners' release, the Irish language and policing. The Belfast Agreement fell well short of the minimum demands that would have to be met before Sinn Féin would sign any agreement[26].

The core of the Belfast Agreement is that in exchange for republican and nationalist *de facto* acceptance of the legitimacy of Northern Ireland's position within the UK and of the principle that the Union will continue as long as a majority of the people in the North support it, and also of the Dublin government's amending of Articles 2 and 3 of its constitution, the British government would replace the Government of Ireland Act and unionists would be required to accept power-sharing with Nationalists in the North as well as cross-border co-operation. Other elements include human rights and equality legislation, prisoner release, policing reform and the decommissioning of weapons[27].

Balanced constitutional changes?

In terms of the central issue of the constitutional position of Northern Ireland and the circumstances in which a united Ireland could be brought about, in the words of constitutional nationalist politician Austin Currie, the Belfast Agreement ensures the Union is 'copper-fastened and protected[28]'. The Belfast Agreement (Strand I, paragraph 33) contains a formal and explicit reiteration of British sovereignty. It states that, 'It is hereby declared that Northern Ireland in its entirety remains part of the United Kingdom and shall not cease to be so without the consent of a majority of the people of Northern Ireland.' (Constitutional Issues, Annex A, Section I, paragraph 1) The British state thus made it clear that the unionist veto shall remain in place and has strengthened the partitionist ethos underlying that veto by having it enshrined in the revised constitution of the 26 counties. (Constitutional Issues, Annex B). The people of Ireland can exercise their right to self-determination but 'this right must be achieved and exercised with and subject to the agreement and consent of a majority of the people of Northern Ireland'. (Constitutional Issues, 1.ii.) This does not incorporate or concede the classic right of self-determination. As legal scholar Austen Morgan notes: 'It is clear that the United Kingdom did not concede that the Irish people (in two states) had a classical right of self-determination. This is evident in the idea of separate referenda in Northern Ireland and the Republic of Ireland, of two conditions precedent to a united Ireland and not simply a numerical majority in an all-Ireland vote[29].'

If the Dublin government had to revise its constitution and revise its territorial claim to the North, according to Sinn Féin thanks to the Belfast Agreement there was no longer any raft of legislation to maintain Northern Ireland as part of the UK, with the British government's repeal of Section 75 of the 1920 Government of Ireland Act. However, the replacement of the 1920 Government of Ireland Act was legally 'of no significance', rather it reconstructed British sovereignty[30]. David Trimble, well read in legal matters, from early on had pointed out that the legislation governing Northern Ireland's place within the UK is the Act of Union of 1800 and the 1973 Constitutional Act, therefore the repeal of Section 75 of the 1920 Government of Ireland Act is legally of no significance.[31] Legally, the Agreement does not shift the balance of constitutional forces towards reunification. The only significant constitutional shift went in the opposite direction, the British state retained sovereignty in the North and the consent principle was embedded, whereas Articles 2 and 3 of the Irish constitution were amended to incorporate the consent principle. Thanks to the framework of the Belfast Agreement, it is the Dublin government, not the British, which has dropped its claim to jurisdiction, leaving Northern Ireland within the UK. The idea that the repeal of Section 75 of the 1920 Government of Ireland Act and amendment of Articles 2 and 3 of the Irish constitution represent some 'balanced constitutional accomodation' as the British and Irish governments put it in their 1998 *Propositions on Heads of Agreement* is an intellectual absurdity.

This represents the best deal unionists could possibly have won and hardly represents a balanced constitutional accomodation. In the words of Tony Blair, the British Prime Minister:

> This offers unionists every key demand they have made since partition eighty years ago...The principle of consent, no change to the constitutional status of Northern Ireland without the consent of the majority of the people, is enshrined. The Irish constitution has been changed...A devolved assembly and government for Northern Ireland is now there for the taking. When I first came to Northern Ireland as a Prime Minister, these demands were pressed in me as what unionists really needed. I have delivered them all[32].

Self-determination or limited form of co-determination?

From a traditional republican point of view, there was a fundamental democratic deficit at the heart of the whole process which led to the 1998 Belfast Agreement. First, it was the British state – democratically unaccountable to any Irish constituency – which determined the parameters of the negotiations, restricting them to those of the Downing Street Declaration, the Framework Document and the Mitchell Principles. The paramount principle espoused in those documents, to which all participants in future talks had to pledge their adherence and commitment, is the principle of consent. Therefore, all participants to the process were committed to partition before the talks commenced. One can thus question the degree to which the Belfast Agreement could be said to have been 'freely negotiated'. Second, the political package on offer was subordinate to the British state's approval. The Belfast Agreement had to be accepted and ratified by Westminster before it was presented to the people of Ireland for acceptance or rejection. An external power had the power of veto over the sovereignty of the people of Ireland, leaving aside any objections they may have. The commitment to the 'people on the island of Ireland alone' is therefore completely meaningless given that there is no self-determination without 'external impediment'.

On 22 May 1998 referenda were held in Northern Ireland and the Republic of Ireland on 'The Agreement' reached during the multi-party talks at Stormont. Many commentators described the referenda as 'historic' as not since the general election of 1918 had the people of Ireland voted on an all-Ireland basis. However, there were two different referenda held on 22 May 1998 in two different states for different purposes and different sets of questions. In the North the people had to vote on the Agreement reached on 10 April, and in the South the electorate was asked to vote on just a few constitutional changes required by that Agreement.

On polling day 22 May, the question on the ballot paper in Northern Ireland was:

'Do you support the Agreement reached at the multi-party talks on Northern Ireland and set out in Command Paper 3883?' [Command Paper 3883 is the technical parliamentary term for the Belfast Agreement]

Turnout was 80.98 per cent of the electorate, with 71.1 per cent voting 'yes' and 28.9 per cent 'no'.

On the same day the electorate of the Republic of Ireland was called to vote on the following question:

'Do you approve of the proposal to amend the Constitution contained in the undermentioned Bill, the Nineteenth Amendment of the Constitution Bill, 1998?'

Turnout was 55.6 per cent of the electorate, with 94.4 per cent voting 'yes' and 5.6 per cent 'no'.

The fact that they were held concurrently did not make them a single event and even less an act of self-determination. As legal scholar Austen Morgan points out: 'It is a travesty to claim that the people of geographical-Ireland voted for the Agreement in an all-Ireland plebiscite[33].' The right to self-determination was fractured. Even Gerry Adams was forced to admit that, 'it is clear that these referenda are not an example of national self-determination[34]'.

The fact that the referenda were carried by a big majority of those who voted in the six counties (71 per cent) and an even larger one in the 26 counties (94.5 per cent) does not refute that there was a democratic deficit at the heart of the whole process:

Given the aggregate preference for Irish unity...the claim

that a single-option referendum that excluded this option from the ballot paper, whatever the pragmatic grounds for its exclusion, constituted a true exercise in Irish self-determination is dubious. Assuming, not unreasonably, that the electoral process is designed to facilitate the unfettered will of the people, a UK election in which the Labour Party appeared as the only choice on the ballot paper could hardly be called a democratic contest. None of this is to dismiss the symbolic importance of both parts of the island voting on essentially the same topic for the first time since 1918, when of course the result of a genuine exercise in Irish self-determination was ignored. Rather it is merely to puncture the grandiose claims made about the 1998 referenda, which in fact were limited exercises in co-determination in that no alternative choices were put to the people, for pragmatic reasons and perhaps for fear of producing the 'wrong' result[35].

Honourable compromise?

The British Prime Minister was quoted as saying the 1998 Agreement offered every key unionist demand they had made since partition; however the Provisional movement claims that the Belfast Agreement does not represent a defeat for republicanism. Danny Morrison, former Sinn Féin publicity director, claims that the British couldn't defeat the IRA nor could the IRA defeat the British, so the IRA did not win but had not lost either[36]. That is demonstrably wrong.

The political objective of the Provisional IRA was to secure a British declaration of intent to withdraw. It failed. The objective of the British state was to force the Provisional IRA to accept – and subsequently respond with a new strategic logic – that it would not leave Ireland until a majority in the North consented to such a move. It succeeded[37].

The Provisional movement claims that the Belfast Agreement does not represent a defeat but an honourable compromise. The problem is less that it is a compromise than the fact that it is a bad compromise[38]. Agnès Maillot is therefore wrong to write that for republicans 'compromise is equated with betrayal[39]'. As a matter of fact, revolutionary movements, as Lenin showed long ago, do not emphatically reject all compromises[40]. There is such a thing as 'revolutionary realpolitik[41]'. It is wrong to frame the republican critique of the Belfast Agreement in terms of absolutism. The fundamental problem is that it was nationalism and republicanism that did the main compromising. Danny Morrison reminds us that among the 'bitter pills the peace process has required republicans to swallow' are:

the deletion of Articles 2 and 3 of the Irish constitution (the territorial claim over the North); the return of a Northern Assembly; Sinn Féin abandoning its traditional policy of abstentionism; reliance on British-government-appointed commissions on the equality and human rights issues and on the future of policing; and the implicit recognition of the principle of unionist consent on the constitutional question[42].

He also adds: 'Republicans sit in an assembly they never wanted. The British government never gave a declaration of intent to withdraw. There is still a heavy British army presence in some nationalist areas. The police have not been reformed. The equality and justice issues have yet to be resolved[43].' 'Yet' as academics Tonge and Murray point out, 'Morrison declined to draw from this catalogue of disasters the conclusion that the peace process was an abject defeat for Republicans[44].' To get a measure of how little has been ceded by unionists – and by implication how much by republicans – we need only view it through the following prism:

If, for example, through the Good Friday Agreement, the unionists had signed up to a British declaration of intent to withdraw from the North and a Dublin declaration of intent to annex the six counties, no amount of wordplay and casuistry would have permitted this outcome to be regarded as anything other than a resounding defeat. Small consolation it would have been to them to have won outright on Strand One matters, such as keeping the RUC intact or the prisoners locked up. Unionism would have lost on the great philosophical question of consent[45].

For all the unionist scepticism about the Belfast Agreement, 'the Unionists have won, they just don't know it[46]'. 'Overall, it would seem that, in terms of the constitutional conflict between nationalism and unionism on the island of Ireland it was the latter that triumphed[47].' Unionists won on the big philosophical issue. In return for unionist concessions on power-sharing and an Irish dimension, nationalism and provisional republicanism explicitly signed up to acknowledging that there can be no end to the Union without the consent of the majority in Northern Ireland, and that it is legitimate for that consent to be withheld if that is the majority view. 'Mr Trimble believes that any nationalist or republican who, accepting the principle of consent, becomes part of the governmental structures within the UK state, is – whatever the genuinely held long-term aspirations – structurally a Unionist[48].' As Eamonn McCann writes: 'Both Republicans and Unionists will have to leave a lot of historical baggage behind in order to make the Belfast Agreement work, and it's the Republicans who'll have to abandon the more valuable items.' That is because while unionists have stuck to their philosophy, 'the Republican leadership have accepted that the Republican analysis is wrong[49]'. Therefore Jonathan Powell is right to note:

The paradox was that it was much harder to sell the Agreement to the unionists than to nationalists and republicans. In many ways republicans had to concede more. After all, if they accepted the principle of consent, that it was for the people of Northern Ireland to decide their future, what had the armed campaign and the suffering been for?[50]

The Provisional movement has gone much further than a 'compromise', an 'accommodation' or a 'negotiated settlement':

In endorsing the 'principle of consent' contained in the Agreement, accepting that Northern Ireland will, as of right, remain part of the United Kingdom until such time as a majority within the six counties decides otherwise, Sinn Féin had ditched the idea that lay at the heart of its own tradition and that had provided the justification in political morality for the campaign, indeed the existence, of the IRA[51].

The Belfast Agreement thus looks more like a republican Versailles than an honourable compromise. 'In trade union terms, the Republican leadership...secured a six-day week and lower wages[52].'

'Sunningdale for slow learners'?

The Belfast Agreement appears even more as a defeat for republicanism if compared to the Sunningdale Agreement 25 years earlier. In December 1973, the SDLP and the Ulster Unionist party had signed up to the Sunningdale Agreement – an arrangement which arguably gave the political parties in Northern Ireland much of what was later on offer in the 1998 Belfast Agreement. Under Sunningdale, power in the province was to be shared by the Northern Ireland executive, with ministers from both the nationalist and unionist communities, and a cross-border Council of Ireland created to stimulate co-operation with the Republic. This is why leading constitutional nationalist politician Seamus Mallon called the Belfast Agreement 'Sunningdale for slow learners[53]'.

The IRA emphatically rejected out of hand this constitutional initiative, viewing it as a British attempt to marginalise republicanism and isolate their struggle. Gerry Adams accused the SDLP, because it had endorsed the arrangement, of being the first Catholic partitionist party[54]. This raises the question of whether the IRA campaign, between its rejection of the Sunningdale Agreement of 1973 and the Belfast Agreement of 1998, was justified given that there is, objectively speaking, very little progress towards republican objectives if the provisions of Sunningdale and the power-sharing executive and the provisions of the Belfast Agreement are compared. Given the similar nature of the two agreements how do the republicans justify not accepting the similar terms on offer at Sunningdale 25 years earlier?

Austin Currie, a minister in the 1974 power-sharing executive, actually feels that in many ways the Sunningdale Agreement was a better deal for nationalists than the Belfast Agreement meaning that the Provisionals finally settled for less than the SDLP got in 1973[55]. If Austin Currie is right, then republicans were wrong to reject Sunningdale for accepting the Belfast Agreement. And if republicans were right to reject Sunningdale, there logically is little justification for them to accept the terms of the Belfast Agreement.

Decommissioning

The 1998 Agreement was, however, more comprehensive than the Sunningdale Agreement as it included also human rights and equality legislation, prisoners release, normalisation of British Army presence, policing reform and the decommissioning of weapons. What do these measures supposed to bring about a 'post-conflict' situation represent?

First, the decommissioning of weapons belonging to illegal

organisations. On Thursday 28 July 2005, the Provisional IRA issued a statement, declaring that its war was over: 'The leadership of Óglaigh na hÉireann has formally ordered an end to the armed campaign. This will take effect from 4pm this afternoon. All IRA units have been ordered to dump arms.' For the first time since 1922, an organisation claiming to be the IRA has publicly declared that there is no need for an armed campaign, as it believes that 'there is an alternative way' to achieve its objectives: namely 'the full implementation of the Good Friday agreement'. This goes much further than a cessation and dumping of arms, which the IRA had done a few times before – in 1922, 1945 and 1962 for instance. 'All volunteers have been instructed to assist the development of purely political and democratic programmes through exclusively peaceful means. Volunteers must not engage in any other activities whatsoever[56].' In other words, 'Now they promise to be nothing more than an old boys' club for former volunteers. As of 4pm yesterday, promised republican Danny Morrison, the IRA will be about as threatening as the British Legion[57].'

Why was that statement issued? There is a fundamental contradiction between accepting the legitimacy of a state, of its laws and institutions, the constitutional system and the rules of parliamentarism and agreeing to operate within their framework; and armed insurrectionary politics dedicated to overthrow them. One cannot accept that the state has the monopoly of legitimate force and at the same time have links to an illegal army refusing to recognise the legitimacy of two governments and ready to kill the servants of both. There is no chance that the unionists would ever consider having Sinn Féin in government as long as they retained links to an illegal organisation carrying out unlawful activities. That is why sooner or later the Provisionals would have to issue such a statement.

Consequently, the statement confirms the Provisional leadership's intent 'to complete the process to verifiably put its arms beyond use in a way which will further enhance public confidence and to conclude this as quickly as possible' and informs that they 'have invited two independent witnesses, from the protestant and catholic churches, to testify to this'. It will thus complete the destruction of its arsenal. After stating on 6 May 2000 that 'the IRA leadership will initiate a process that will completely and verifiably put IRA arms beyond use', on 23 October 2001, it began the destruction of its stock of weaponry; and on 17 September 2005 completed the process.

The political significance of decommissioning is crucial. It showed that the Provisional IRA war was truly over – an army does not destroy its weapons if it is to fight a war. It was an act of surrender. There has never been a situation in the world where an 'undefeated army' has willingly and unilaterally handed over its weapons to its enemy. The only situation where that applies is when an army has been defeated and is forced to hand over arms as an act of surrender. In this context it is interesting to note that in 2000 Nelson Mandela stated not being in favour of the IRA decommissioning[58]. Critics also pointed out that the acceptance of the principle of decommissioning has served to de-legitimise and criminalise the previous republican resistance to British rule. It also elevates to a higher moral plateau British state weaponry. 'Basically republicans are being told that the weapons used by Francis Hughes, the deceased hunger striker, to kill a member of the British SAS death squad are contaminated in a manner which the weapons used to slaughter the innocent of Bloody Sunday and the victims of shoot-to-kill are not[59]'. This was historically unique:

Never before in the long and bloody history of Anglo-Irish conflict had an Irish insurgent group voluntarily given up its weapons for destruction, even self-destruction, at the behest of its opponents. When de Valera recognised the inevitability of defeat in the terrible Irish civil war and called a halt to the

IRA's campaign in May 1923, the organisation was ordered to bury its arms, not to destroy them. Similarly, when the 1956-1962 Border Campaign ended, Ruairí Ó Brádaigh's last order to the IRA units as chief of staff was to 'dump arms'[60].

One just has to look at what the IRA constitution has to say to realise the extent of the shift taken by the Provisionals:

General Order No. 11 (Deals with the seizure of arms and dumps under Army control.)

a) Any volunteer who seizes or is party to the seizure of arms, ammunition or explosives which are being held under Army control shall be deemed guilty of treason. A duly-constituted court martial shall try all cases.

Penalty for breach of this order: Death.

The deed was done and General Order No. 11 was breached coldly, deliberately and publicly. William Shakespeare once asked: 'When is treason not treason?' Answer: 'When it is successful; because then none dare call it treason.' But those who went before us would dare[61].

The decommissioning of IRA weapons appears even more unilateral as it was not before 3 May and 11 November 2007 that the illegal Loyalist paramilitary groups the UVF and UDA declared their war to be over and it was only on 8 February 2010 that the decommissioning of their weapons was completed. As opposed to the Provisional IRA, their decommissioning was not an act of political surrender. When on 3 May 2007 the UVF declared its war to be over, it stated that 'the constitutional question has now been firmly settled' as 'the principle of consent has been firmly established and...the Union remains safe'. The organisation also 'accepts as significant support by the mainstream republican movement of the constitutional status quo'. Contrary to the IRA, Loyalists have achieved their political objectives[62].

Troops out?

The decommissioning of weapons held by illegal organisations is to be differentiated from the downsizing of the British Army and reducing the extent of the security apparatus in Northern Ireland. The Agreement aimed to normalise the exceptional security arrangements that existed in Northern Ireland in 1998. It committed the UK government to making 'progress towards the objective of as early a return as possible to normal security arrangements'. A total of 15,500 British soldiers were deployed in Northern Ireland at the time of the 1998 Agreement but on 1 August 2007 only a garrison force of 5000 soldiers remained. At the end of 1999, there remained 19 towers and observation posts, 32 bases and military installations, and 20 joint RUC and British Army sites. By 31 July 2007, all bases and installations had been closed except for 12 core sites. The UK government ended the military's campaign in Northern Ireland – Operation Banner, during which over 250,000 troops had been deployed – on 31 July 2007.

In 2007, an internal document of the British Army stated that its campaign against the IRA was brought to a 'successful conclusion'. The document, *Operation Banner: an Analysis of Military Operations in Northern Ireland* by General Sir Mike Jackson, was released by the Ministry of Defence following a request under the Freedom of Information Act. Jackson said the army's campaign in the North was 'one of the very few ever brought to a successful conclusion by the armed forces of a developed nation against an irregular force'.

Section Eight of the document states:

It should be recognised that the Army did not 'win' in any recognisable way; rather it achieved its desired end-state, which allowed a political process to be established without unacceptable levels of intimidation. Security force operations suppressed the level of violence to a level which the population could live with, and with which the RUC and, later, the Police Service of Northern Ireland (PSNI) could cope. The violence was reduced to an extent which made it clear to the PIRA that they would not win through violence. This is a major achievement and one with which the security forces from all three services, with the Army in the lead, should be entirely satisfied[63].

The British Army ended Operation Banner as it had successfully achieved its aims. It marked the ends of this operation, but not the end of the British Army's presence in Northern Ireland as a garrison of 5000 permanent troops remains. Depending on the perceived level of threat, more troops can be brought back anytime, as the case of units of the Special Reconnaissance Regiment brought back from Iraq and Afghanistan to Northern Ireland illustrates[64]. After the end of Operation Banner on 31 July 2007, Operation Helvetic began on 1 August 2007. Under this new operation, the armed forces which remained in Northern Ireland continued to provide specialist support to the police[65]. The British government has been much less successful in reducing the *role* of the army than it has in removing security installations and reducing troop numbers. The Independent Monitoring Commission, which among other things monitored between 2004 and 2011 the commitment by the British government to a package of security normalisation measures, made an important observation when stating in one of its reports that 'such a role [for the armed forces] would be abnormal elsewhere in the UK'. On top of that, garrisoned troops in Northern Ireland have additional powers that those in the rest of the UK do not. 'The partial implementation of the Agreement's programme of security normalisation has not ensured that Northern Ireland has become a normal part of the UK; the powers granted to the armed forces in Northern Ireland are still exceptional[66].' Reducing troop levels does not mean 'troops out'...

71

RUC disbanded?

But in periods of 'peace', the main repressive state apparatus is the police rather than the army. Until 1998 four essential features distinguished the RUC from police forces elsewhere in the United Kingdom. First, its job of 'ordinary' policing was subordinate to the tasks of counter-insurgency. Second, it was not seen as representative of the population as a whole as nationalists were significantly under-represented and the force suffered from legitimacy deficit and a lack of trust among that section of the population. Third, there were questions as to how accountable the force was. People have found it extremely difficult to secure protection and redress in the courts against police excesses. Fourth, the RUC operated in a particularly dangerous environment, with Northern Ireland being the most dangerous place in the world to be a police officer. According to Interpol figures, the risk factor in 1983 was twice as high as in El Salvador, the second-most dangerous. During the conflict the RUC lost 300 officers (199 full-time constables and 101 reservists), 87 of them while off duty and a further 19 were killed after having retired from the force. Due to these extraordinary features, the Belfast Agreement promised policing reform and the Patten Commission released its report and 175 recommendations on the future of policing in Northern Ireland on 9 September 1999. As a result of the Patten recommendations for a new departure in policing, the new PSNI came into being on 4 November 2001. Close to 20 years after Patten, to what extent has policing in Northern Ireland been transformed?

Policing is still a contentious issue. In terms of composition, if in 1998 there were 8.3 per cent of Catholics in the RUC, thanks to 50-50 recruitment 31.5 per cent of the force are Catholic in 2018, but a more representative figure based on demographics would be about 45 per cent[67]. But a university study has emphasised that these were not typical or representative of their community[68]. Moreover, among those who resigned from the PSNI between

2001 and 2011, 56.2 per cent were Catholics compared to 39.4 per cent Protestants. The proportion of Catholics in the prisons in Northern Ireland is twice that within the PSNI. Trust in the police force remains lower among the Catholic population (72 per cent) than among the Protestant population (81 per cent) and is lower than elsewhere in the United Kingdom[69]. The issue of how representative the PSNI is of the overall population is thus not entirely settled.

Due to the 'security situation', during the 1980s there were 8.4 members of the security forces for every 1000 people in Northern Ireland; this compared to 1.6 in France for example[70]. Despite the 'end of the conflict', Northern Ireland remains heavily policed. At the end of 2013 there were 6860 police officers in the six counties, which represents one officer for every 265 people; whereas in the rest of the UK the proportion is one officer for every 436 people and in the 26 counties one for every 344 people. This despite crime rates being lower in the six counties than elsewhere in the UK and the 26 counties[71]. Whereas police forces elsewhere in the British Isles are not usually armed, the PSNI remains militarised. Police stations are fortified and PSNI officers move around in PANGOLIN land rovers and since December 2007 constantly wear bullet-proof jackets. The PSNI also has powers for the purposes of countering terrorism that other police services in Britain do not have. This is not the only way in which the PSNI remains exceptional from other UK police forces. It continues to operate as a routinely armed police service and has a broad plethora of arms at its disposal including firearms, CS spray, water cannon, Attenuating Energy Projectiles and Tasers not used elsewhere in the UK[72]. The degree to which counter-insurgency tasks predominate over 'ordinary' policing can be measured by the proportion of its budget devoted to 'security costs'. In 2016, 27 per cent of the PSNI's budget, or £297 million, was spent on 'policing the security situation'[73]. Security costs were defined as those unique costs incurred by the PSNI, over and above normal policing costs, as a direct result of the specific security situation in Northern Ireland now or in the past. It is unlikely that any other police force elsewhere in the UK spends such a large proportion of its budget on 'security' costs.

While a Police Ombudsman has been set up to investigate complaints against the PSNI, its credibility was heavily damaged by a report published in 2011 criticising the extent to which it is effectively independent. District Policing Partnerships have been set up to encourage the idea that the PSNI is accountable to the public. However, the PSNI has the right to refuse commenting on issues it regards as 'sensitive', which indicates that its accountability remains limited. There is also the whole issue of closed material procedures that also indicates a lack of accountability[74].

Moreover, on 25 February 2005 the British government decreed that from 10 October 2007 in certain matters, the role of the PSNI will be entirely subordinated to national security bodies like MI5 which themselves are not accountable to the public. A new MI5 base was opened on 4 December 2007 in Loughside, Palace Barracks, Holywood, outside Belfast. Employing over 400 people, it is the most important of the eight MI5 bases outside of Thames House (its London headquarters). The role of British secret services has in fact significantly increased in Northern Ireland since 2007. In 2018 15 per cent of MI5's total budget is spent on operations there.

Logically, once the Provisionals agreed not to oppose the armed forces of the state, they would have to explicitly accept the state's monopoly of armed force and agree to observe its laws. In practice, this means supporting the police forces north and south of the border that they had been fighting for more than 3 decades. There was a contradiction with the fact that while the party was prepared to administer British rule, it refused to accept British policing structures in the North. The party cannot have ministers making the laws and at the same time refuse to endorse the forces in charge of implementing them. This was an absurd and illogical political position. One either rejects the legitimacy of a state or accepts it. One cannot reject the legitimacy of one arm of the state and accept the legitimacy of another.

The 1998 Belfast Agreement made it quite clear that signatories would have to accept new internal policing arrangements. The Provisional movement had to accept the state's monopoly of legitimate violence. On 28 January 2007, a Sinn Féin Ard Fheis made the 'historic' decision to support the PSNI and the criminal justice system; appoint party representatives to the Policing Board and District Policing Partnership Boards; and actively encourage everyone in the community to co-operate fully with the police services in tackling crime in all areas and actively support all the criminal justice institutions. The Provisionals have even asked for a special unit to be set up by the PSNI to combat so-called dissidents[75]. For all the hopes of Sinn Féin to one day control the justice ministry, the transfer of 'counter-terrorist' intelligence from the police to MI5 means at present that any justice minister would have no effective control over counter-terrorist operations in Northern Ireland. Sinn Féin is colluding with the British state to hide the fact that MI5 has been given an expanded role in the North to take supreme control of all counter-terrorist intelligence with virtually no accountability or outside control and when justice is set to be devolved, control of security matters will remain at Westminster.

Removal of emergency powers?

Since its very inception, Northern Ireland has been governed by emergency laws: the 1922 Civil Authorities (Special Powers) Act, replaced by the Northern Ireland (Emergency Provisions) Act 1973 and the Prevention of Terrorism (Temporary Provisions) Act 1974 which have been renewed every year until 1998. Those emergency laws were heavily criticised by civil liberties and human rights organisations. The Belfast Agreement promised to remove them and they were replaced by the Terrorism Act 2000, voted for on 20 July 2000, the Terrorism (Northern Ireland) Act 2006 and the Justice and Security (Northern Ireland) Act voted for on 24 May 2007. Technically these Acts replaced the previous emergency legislation but re-created it under another form incorporating the panoply of repressive laws introduced after 9-11[76]. As Jessie Blackbourn puts it:

The recent enactment by the UK government of a vast regime of permanent anti-terrorism laws for the whole of the UK, including Northern Ireland, has meant that for the most part Northern Ireland is no longer an outlier. Northern Ireland is a normal part of the UK's anti-terrorism regime. However, this has come at the cost of the adoption by the rest of the UK of exceptional anti-terrorism powers that once were reserved solely for terrorism in Northern Ireland. A normalisation has therefore occurred, but it is not the one envisioned by the Agreement[77].

On top of that a number of Northern Ireland's exceptional anti-terrorism measures were transferred into the ordinary criminal law, including the controversial provision for non-jury trial.

From the year 2006/2007 until the end of 2014/2015 there were a total of 1748 arrests under terror laws in Northern Ireland, resulting in 399 persons charged, 80 convicted and just 48 jailed[78]. In November 2012, the Committee on the Administration of Justice in a report argued that on occasions the PSNI used stop and search legislation not to search for weapons for example, but for the 'disruption' of persons suspected to be 'dissident' republicans. Section 44 of the Terrorism Act 2000 allows the PSNI to stop and search people without 'reasonable suspicion'. The code of practice which governs the use of the Terrorism Act 2000 (TACT) specifically bars the use of stop and search as a 'deterrent or intelligence gathering tool'. Since a European court declared Section 44 contrary to its principles, Section 24 of the Justice and Security Act (JSA) – which has similar scope to Section 44 – empowered the PSNI to stop and search without reasonable suspicion as a criterion. In one year, the number of people stopped under Section 44 jumped from 1163 to 16,023 – a 1277 per cent increase[79]! The arrest rate in JSA cases is significantly lower than in Police and Criminal Evidence Order cases where reasonable suspicion is required. The arrest rate following stop and search is very low in Northern Ireland – in 2012/2013 it was below 6 per cent, even lower than the 9 per cent in England and Wales which the Home Secretary has deemed unacceptable. This suggests stop and search is used for political harassment. At the time of writing, a case was pending at the High Court in Belfast in which the applicant, Steven Ramsey from Derry, who said he had been stopped 200 times in 5 years, would claim that the Section 24/schedule 3 power was incompatible with Article 8 of the European Convention on Human Rights (right to respect for private and family life). His case centres on stop and search actions carried out under the Justice and Security (NI) Act 2007. He claimed he was subjected to 35 searches in 2009, 37 in 2010, another 23 in 2011, 31 in 2012 and a further 30 up to August 2013. This is an indication of what republicans have called 'political policing'. 'Political policing' may be said to exist when some are either over-policed or under-policed for political rather than legal reasons as Anthony McIntyre once defined it.

Some will argue that all the 'exceptional' ('abnormal' others would say) features of policing described above are in fact a normal and legitimate response to the level of threat faced today by police officers in Northern Ireland who have been targeted on and off duty by republicans continuing the armed struggle. Two of the 16 PSNI officers who have lost their lives in the line of duty since 2001 have been killed by such republicans. It is interesting that in 2018, 'as the 20th anniversary of the signing of the Belfast Agreement approaches, one of the first things PSNI recruits are still taught is how to check under their cars for explosive devices[80']. If faced with a situation like that in which officers Carroll and Kerr lost their lives, any other police force in liberal-democratic countries would resort to similar measures. If there were no armed actions by republicans today there would not be a need for the PSNI to be the way it is or for such repressive legislation.

The weakness of that argument is that the British state has historically not been able to rule any part of Ireland 'normally' as its very presence was contested by some section of the population. Between 1800 and 1921, there were 105 Coercion Acts initiated by Britain in Ireland and during the first half century after the 1800 Act of Union, Ireland was ruled by the ordinary law of the land for only 5 years. Since its inception, because Northern Ireland has lacked sufficient political legitimacy it has been bolstered by an array of repressive measures which have been largely introduced to police and regulate the sizeable nationalist population within its borders.

Legal mechanisms such as the Civil Authorities (Special Powers) Act 1922, replaced by the Northern Ireland (Emergency Provisions) Act 1973 and the Prevention of Terrorism Act 1974 and later by the current anti-terrorist legislation, have provided for a range of measures which have been at odds with practices in western liberal-democratic states. The exceptional features of policing in Northern Ireland today are illustrative of the fact that despite the peace process many components of the state in Northern Ireland have never been able to function in a 'normal' way.

Prisoners release

The 1998 Agreement allowed the early release of what remained in 1998 of the people imprisoned as a result of the conflict. As a result of this, between 11 September 1998 and 28 July 2000, 447 prisoners benefited from an early release scheme in the

North: 241 republicans, 194 Loyalists, as well as 12 non-aligned prisoners. Parallel to this, 57 republicans imprisoned in the South also benefited from an early release scheme. On 29 September 2000, HMP The Maze (also known as Long Kesh and famous for its H-Blocks) closed for good and began to be demolished on 30 October 2006.

It is important to emphasise that there was no amnesty following the 1998 Agreement, but a conditional and revocable early release scheme. According to the Northern Ireland (Sentences) Act 1998, people who are released from prison – whether after the 1998 Agreement or before – can always have their licence revoked if the British state decides to. That there was no amnesty is also shown by the fact that the British state continues to prosecute people for incidents related to the 1969-1998 conflict[81]. In 2018 over one-third of killings carried out in Northern Ireland during the conflict – 1186 – are still being investigated by police.

The early release of prisoners following the 1998 Agreement could give the impression that the issue is now solved. But the problem is that there continues to be republican prisoners, even though they are far fewer in numbers than during the 1969-1998 period. Approximately 300 republicans have been imprisoned between 1999 and 2009 in the north and south of Ireland and elsewhere. In 2018 there remains less than a hundred republican prisoners, mostly in Portlaoise prison in the South and Maghaberry prison in the North. In the North, political prisoners currently represent less than 5 per cent of the prison population. The British state has decided to abolish all gains and privileges won by republican prisoners during the conflict, and has attempted to treat republicans imprisoned after the 1998 Agreement as ordinary criminals. This has given rise to a number of struggles in the prison since 1999. As earlier in the conflict, republican prisoners were on dirty protest from 4 April to 12 August 2010, as well as from 6 May 2011 to 20 November 2012 to protest against 23 hours lock-up and body searches[82]. Cells and wings have been damaged, walls daubed with human faeces and prisoners have gone on dirty protest, all of which conjure up images of the 1981 H-Blocks hunger strikes when ten men died, and the years before. As a result of the problems in Maghaberry, two prison officers were killed outside by republicans. The prison system was not reformed after the 1998 Agreement and an official report deemed prison conditions 'oppressive'. If in Great Britain there is an average of three prison guards for every 12 prisoners, in Northern Ireland the average is five guards for every three prisoners. In November 2015, Northern Ireland's Inspectorate of Prisons and Criminal Justice described Maghaberry as Victorian and Dickensian, 'unsafe and unstable' and 'in crisis'. This is why the *Irish Times* was right to conclude in 2017 that the prison system in the North had been 'left behind by peace[83]'.

Human rights

The Belfast Agreement in 1998 contained a comprehensive set of human rights safeguards. These included the introduction of the European Convention on Human Rights (ECHR) to be accessible in Northern Ireland courts, establishment of the Northern Ireland Human Rights Commission, consultation by the commission on any additional rights supplementary to the ECHR to constitute a Bill of Rights, and prohibition of the Northern Ireland Assembly to legislate in any way contrary to the ECHR or any Bill of Rights. But a recent legal study laments that the promises of the Belfast Agreement regarding human rights have not yet been fully realised and remain 'an unfulfilled agenda[84]'. A Northern Ireland Human Rights Commission came into existence on 1 March 1999. But the incorporation into Northern Ireland law of the ECHR is now endangered by Brexit[85] and the UK government has not yet enacted a Bill of Rights.

If from a general point of view human rights remain an unfulfilled agenda, the particular experience of republicans shows that the 1998 Agreement has failed to prevent human rights abuses as the effective return of internment without trial demonstrates. The case of Marian Price is the most famous instance of this. She was arrested and imprisoned on 13 May 2011 on the basis of no criminal charges and without a trial. She was held in solitary confinement and was only released on 30 May 2013 following an important campaign of mobilisation after her health significantly deteriorated as a result of her incarceration. Her case joins that of former republican prisoner Martin Corey. On 16 April 2010 he was arrested and imprisoned without charge or trial. The Court of Appeal ordered his release on 9 July 2012, but it was not until 15 January 2014 that he was released under very strict conditions. Republican activist Stephen Murney was interned without charge nor trial between 29 November 2012 and 24 February 2014 before being cleared of any wrong doing by the courts. Tony Taylor has in May 2018 spent over 800 days in jail despite not having been charged with any fresh offences. Mr Taylor, a former spokesman for the Republican Network for Unity, was arrested on 10 March 2016, the day after the former Secretary of State for the North revoked his release licence. The fact that 20 years after the 1998 Agreement people can be effectively interned without trial – contrary to all domestic and international human rights standards – shows that human rights remain an unresolved issue in the North. One should also mention the case of the so-called 'Craigavon Two', sentenced to life imprisonment for the killing of a police officer in 2009. There are serious grounds to think that this is a miscarriage of justice, like the Guildford Four and Birmingham Six had been decades earlier[86].

'Remarkable progress' or 'Back where we started in 1969'?

For Gerry Adams:

Unlike the efforts that governments had concocted before –

from Sunningdale in December 1973 through to the Anglo-Irish Agreement in 1985 – the Good Friday Agreement was genuinely comprehensive and inclusive and addressed the broad range of issues that had been previously ignored... It secured remarkable progress in the areas of policing and justice, demilitarisation and arms, discrimination and sectarianism, equality, human rights and the Irish language. The underlying ethos of the agreement and the major difference between it and all its predecessors is that equality lies at its core[87].

This is to be contrasted with what an IRA spokesperson stated in 1975: 'Suppose we get the release of all detainees, an amnesty and withdrawal of troops to barracks, we are still where we started in 1969[88].' All these developments represent strategic progress for the British state. In January 1976, a commission headed by Sir John Bourne produced an important document entitled *The Way Ahead*. It recommended the reduction of the army presence and police primacy for counter-insurgency tasks ('Ulsterisation'), treating republican prisoners like ordinary criminals ('Criminalisation') in order to give public opinion the impression that the situation in Northern Ireland had become normal again ('Normalisation'). After examining above the issues of policing and justice, demilitarisation and arms and human rights, it is difficult to avoid the conclusion that if the 1998 Agreement 'secured remarkable progress' in something, it is in advancing the 'ulsterisation', 'criminalisation' and 'normalisation' agenda of the British state. Republicans, however, are closer to where they started in 1969 than to achieving their aims.

Movement is everything

On 10 May 1998 the Belfast Agreement was approved 331 for and only 19 against at a special Sinn Féin conference. To endorse the Agreement, 'we went to a special Ard Fheis of our party, and then we went to another special Ard Fheis of our party and we turned policy on its head[89]', recalled Gerry Adams later. How can one explain that as Danny Morrison points out, the bulk of 'relatives of dead IRA volunteers, former hunger strikers, ex-escapees, former prisoners, as well as thousands of supporters[90]' remained supporters of the Provisional movement and its leadership despite it turning republicanism on its head? It is 'thanks to the loyalty factor' as Brendan Hughes pointed out. Loyalty to the movement is a decisive factor. 'The response to democratic republicanism has always been a plea to stay within the army line...The republican leadership has always exploited our loyalty,' noted Brendan Hughes in a famous interview[91]. With such a mindset, that the movement must remain united becomes an imperative[92]. Years later, some prominent republicans declared that they had had fundamental objections to Sinn Féin's political strategy for a long time but that they and others remained loyal to the leadership to avoid splitting the movement[93]. This is evidence of the primacy of organisational unity over unity around political principles. It is the Irish version of the social democratic maxim 'the movement is everything and the principles nothing[94]'. Once the movement is more important than principles, republicanism becomes whatever the leadership of the movement said it is. 'Thus Republicanism that declared "No Return to Stormont" in 1997 was still Republicanism when it meant Executive ministries at Stormont in 1999[95].' The intervention of prisoners in support of the leadership was also important. Had the Provisionals not backed the Belfast Agreement, the prisoners aligned to the movement would have had to spend long years in jail.

Principles and tactics

In terms of international comparison, journalist Kevin Rafter cannot find any other example of political movements who have gone so far in the dilution of their core principles: 'No other political party in Europe has undergone such a radical overhaul of its basic principles, not even the former communist parties in Central and Eastern Europe that transformed themselves into social democratic entities in the aftermath of the fall of the Soviet bloc.' More significantly, in an Irish context, there are no historical precedents of a republican organisation going so far[96]. The leadership of the Provisional movement succeeded in convincing their base that their dilution of core principles was not a dilution of 'principles' but just of 'tactics'. The outcome of deliberately confusing 'principles' and 'tactics' is a situation where there are no longer any principles, but just tactics. 'The record of the Adams era shows that everything in the republican code is now a tactic...He has displayed a total disregard for traditional republican dogma and has refused to be hamstrung by historical principles[97].'

Pragmatism or opportunism?

The Provisionals' ideological retreat has often been explained in terms of 'pragmatism' and 'recognizing realities'. The Sandinistas had been a source of inspiration for Irish republicans and when they lost the elections in Nicaragua in 1990, Danny Morrison drew the following lesson: 'The Sandinistas had to come to terms with reality. The pragmatism of the head had to take precedence over the principle of the heart.[98]' Shortly before his death in 2008, prominent IRA leader Brian Keenan stated: 'Revolutionaries have to be pragmatic – wish lists are for Christmas.[99]' According to the 'pragmatist' thesis: 'The trade-off has been between a position of principle combined with isolation or opting for pragmatism married to political success. In the "era of pragmatism", the Adams leadership ensured which choice was made[100].' In an important article Danny Morrison argues:

There are many republicans who feel that the IRA leadership went too far...I myself think that while there have been mistakes they got the balance just about right. But it has been

84

a difficult road given that the armed struggle was waged – and could only have been waged – with idealistic zeal and for fundamental demands...Life is complex, circumstances change, battles are won and lost, opportunities arise, and, as in nature, it is those who can adapt who survive and thrive. In fact, to use and exploit the system in a considered way, both in its contradictions or whatever advantages it offers to achieve one's ultimate aims is often to do the revolutionary thing. And this, to me, is the story of the peace process, and the peace process to me is a phase of struggle.[101]

The problem with this argument is that it tends to confuse pragmatism and opportunism. Pragmatism is about temporarily setting aside a minor ideal to achieve some higher ideal. Opportunism is abandoning some important political principles in the process of trying to increase one's political power and influence. With pragmatism, there is unity between means and ends; whereas with opportunism, political means have become ends in themselves and the original relation between means and ends is lost. Political circumstances change and so do tactics, but tactical flexibility is still connected to the strategic goals of the programme. Only when tactics are applied in a manner that undermines the realisation of strategic aims can they be said to be unprincipled. The confusion of principles and tactics opens the road to opportunism[102].

As with the PLO under Arafat, one can see with Sinn Féin that 'premature compromises on matters of principle have made the word "peace" synonymous with giving up before getting anything[103]'.

Regarding the issue of 'pragmatism' and 'recognising realities', Joseph A. Massad emphasises that: 'The new value system stresses "nation-building" as opposed to national liberation, "liberal democracy" as opposed to resistance, "pragmatism" as opposed to utopianism and, finally, "realism" as opposed to nostalgia[104].' Those who speak of the 'realism' of Sinn Féin are not realists at all. Their fantastic schemes demonstrate that political 'realism' is an effect of the dominant discourse that they fail to question. As Edward W. Said put it: 'It is simply not enough to say that we live in the New World Order which requires "pragmatism" and "realism" and that we must shed the old ideas of nationalism and liberation. That is pure nonsense. No outside power like Israel or the United States can unilaterally decree what reality is[105].' But Sinn Féin accepts 'reality' as it is defined by the British state and its allies, hence its 'pragmatism' and 'realism'.

Conclusion

In an article published in 1999 in *Le Monde Diplomatique* newspaper to mark the first anniversary of the Belfast Agreement, Robbie McVeigh spoke of 'unfinished decolonisation in Northern Ireland[106]'. A few years later, the same author concluded that in terms of self-determination, the peace process had transformed Northern Ireland into some kind of Bantustan[107]. This sets the terms of the debate regarding what the process had achieved: at best unfinished decolonisation, at worst some Bantustan. Like in the Middle-East, its defenders were quick 'to proclaim defeat a victory, metamorphose weakness into strength, and surrender into bravery[108]'. Martin Mansergh, a Fianna Fáil politician who played a leading role in the peace process, noted that the whole premise of it was that 'no side had "won", no side had "lost", and no side was "surrendering"[109]'. This chapter attempted to demonstrate how wrong this idea is. The 1998 Agreement fractures the right of self-determination of the people of Ireland as a whole. The sovereignty of the British state has been reinforced. Not only does this represent a defeat for Irish republicanism, but Sinn Féin has joined the enemy camp. The Provisional movement had gone from being the vanguard of the historic struggle for an independent, 32-county republic to a counter-revolutionary barrier protecting the British presence in Ireland. Sinn Féin has been de-republicanised and the entire liberation project has been weakened as it now accepts the political terms of its opponent. The result of the process is less a case of 'one step forward' than 'two steps backwards'.

Endnotes

1   Richard J. Harvey (1990), The Right of the People of the Whole of Ireland to Self-Determination, Unity, Sovereignty and Independence, *New York Law School Journal of International and Comparative Law*, 11, 167-206

2   Claire Hackett (1995), Self-Determination: The Republican Feminist Agenda, *Feminist Review*, 50, 111-116

3   Bill Kissane (2003), The doctrine of self-determination and the Irish move to independence, 1916-1922, *Journal of Political Ideologies*, 8:3, 327-346

4   For a thought-provoking discussion of this issue see: Anthony Carty (1996), *Was Ireland Conquered? International Law and the Irish Question*, London: Pluto Press

5   Amy Maguire (2013), Contemporary Anti-Colonial Self-Determination Claims and the Decolonisation of International Law, *Griffith Law Review*, 22:1, 238-268

6   For the IRA's demands see *Hansard* 840 (10 July 1972), col. 1179-1180; Seán Mac Stíofáin (1975), *Memoirs of a Revolutionary*, Edinburgh: Gordon Cremonesi, 282; Daithi Ó Conaill, Three Basic War Aims, *Republican News*, 5 August 1978

7   See: *Northern Ireland Constitution Act 1973*, London: Her Majesty's Stationery Office, 18 July 1973; *Northern Ireland Constitutional Proposals*, London: Her Majesty's Stationery Office, 20 March 1973, Cmnd. 5259; and *The Future of Northern Ireland, A Paper for Discussion*, Belfast: Northern Ireland Office, Her Majesty's Stationery Office, 30 October

1972

8   Roger Mac Ginty, Rick Wilford, Lizanne Dowds and Gillian Robinson (2001), Consenting Adults: The Principle of Consent and Northern Ireland's Constitutional Future, *Government and Opposition*, 36:4, 472-492

9   Brian P. Murphy (1996), Peace Talks and Majority Consent: An Historical Perspective, *Studies: An Irish Quarterly Review*, 85:340, 311-322

10 *Hansard*, sixth series, vol.231, col.35

11 Anthony Bevins, Eamonn Mallie and Mary Holland, Major's secret links with IRA leadership revealed, *The Observer*, 28 November 1993

12 Anthony McIntyre, Why Stormont Reminded me of Animal Farm, *Sunday Tribune*, 12 April 1998

13 Anthony McIntyre, Sinn Féin stance hinders Republican cause, *Sunday Tribune*, 20 July 1997. The same expression is also the title of a former IRA volunteer's recollections of the period: Matt Treacy (2017), *A Tunnel to the Moon: The End of the Irish Republican Army*, Dublin: Brocaire Books

14 David Trimble, Ulster's Lesson for the Middle East: don't indulge extremists, *The Guardian*, 25 October 2007

15 *Hansard*, sixth series, vol. 234 col. 1072-3

16 Peter Taylor (1998), *The Provos: the IRA and Sinn Féin*, London: Bloomsbury, 343

17 *Hansard*, sixth series, vol. 255 col. 358

18 Henry McDonald (2008), *Gunsmoke and Mirrors: How Sinn Féin dressed up defeat as victory*, Dublin: Gill & Macmillan, 154-155

19 John Bew, Martyn Frampton, and Iñigo Gurruchaga (2009), *Talking to Terrorists: Making Peace in Northern Ireland and the Basque Country*, London: Hurst & Company, 133-134

20 Another chance for progress, *An Phoblacht-Republican News*, 24 July 1997

21 Jonathan Powell (2008), *Great Hatred, Little Room. Making*

Peace in Northern Ireland, London: The Bodley Head, 23

22   Jonathan Powell, op.cit., 11-12 and 79-80

23   Brendan Ó Muirthile, Strategic Republicanism: Neither strategic nor republican, *The Blanket* website, January 2002

24   See: Thomas Hennessey (2009), Negotiating the Belfast Agreement, in: Brian Barton and Patrick J. Roche (eds), *The Northern Ireland Question: The Peace Process and the Belfast Agreement*, Basingstoke: Palgrave Macmillan, 38-56

25   Paul Bew (2007), *Ireland: The Politics of Enmity 1789-2006*, Oxford University Press, 549

26   Among the 'minimum' criteria were powerful cross-border bodies immune from the Northern Assembly, the disbandment of the RUC and no weakening of Dublin's constitutional claim to the North. See for example: *Peace in Ireland: Freedom, Justice, Democracy, Equality*. Submissions from Sinn Féin to talks process at Stormont September 1997 to March 1998, published April 1998

27   For the full text of the Agreement and an in-depth discussion of its constitutional and legal aspects see in particular: Austen Morgan (2000), *The Belfast Agreement: A Practical Legal Analysis*, London: The Belfast Press

28   Austin Currie (2004), *All Hell Will Break Loose*, Dublin: O'Brien Press, 434

29   Austen Morgan (2009), The Belfast Agreement and the Constitutional Status of Northern Ireland, in B. Barton and P. J. Roche (eds), op.cit., 86

30   Brigid Hadfield (1998), The Belfast Agreement, Sovereignty and the State of the Union, *Public Law*, volume 15: Winter, 615

31   Thomas Hennessey (2000), *The Northern Ireland Peace Process: Ending the Troubles?*, Dublin: Gill & Macmillan, 139-145

32   Tony Blair, A historic opportunity that Northern Ireland cannot afford to miss, *Sunday Times*, 4 July 1999

33   Austen Morgan, The Belfast Agreement and the Constitutional Status of Northern Ireland, op.cit., 90

34   Address by Sinn Féin president Gerry Adams at 1998 Ard Fheis, *An Phoblacht-Republican News*, 14 May 1998

35   Jonathan Tonge (2005), *The New Northern Irish Politics?*, Hampshire: Palgrave Macmillan, 49-50

36   Danny Morrison, The war is over...Now we must look for the future, *The Guardian*, 11 May 1998

37   Anthony McIntyre, We, the IRA, have failed, *The Guardian*, 22 May 1998

38   Gerry Ruddy (2003), The Good Friday Agreement – revisited, in: *Models of Governance: The Good Friday Agreement and Beyond*, Coiste na n-Iarchimí, Belfast, 5

39   Agnès Maillot (2005), *New Sinn Féin: Irish republicanism in the twenty-first century*, London and New York: Routledge, 174

40   Cfr. 'No Compromises?' in *Left Wing Communism, an Infantile Disorder*, V.I. Lenin (1966), Collected Works: Volume 31, Moscow: Progress Publishers, 66ff

41   Georg Lukács (1970), *Lenin: A Study in the Unity of his Thought*, London: NLB, 72ff

42   Danny Morrison, Stretching Republicans Too Far, *The Guardian*, 13 July 1999

43   Danny Morrison, Get on with the business of peace, *The Guardian*, 14 October 2002

44   Gerard Murray and Jonathan Tonge (2005), *Sinn Féin and the SDLP From Alienation to Participation*, London: Hurst & Company, 234

45   Anthony McIntyre (2001), Modern Irish Republicanism and the Belfast Agreement: chickens coming home to roost, or turkeys celebrating Christmas? in: Rick Wilford (ed) *Aspects of the Belfast Agreement*, Oxford University Press, 217

46   Paul Bew (2007), *The Making and Remaking of the Good Friday*

Agreement, Dublin: The Liffey Press, 28, 100

47 Thomas Hennessey (2009), Negotiating the Belfast Agreement, in: Brian Barton and Patrick J. Roche (eds), op.cit., 55-56. David Trimble himself wondered whether the scale of his victory might not be too great to the point where the Provisional leadership might not be able to endorse the 1998 deal. Cfr. Dean Godson (2004), *Himself Alone: David Trimble and the Ordeal of Unionism,* London: Harper Collins, 326-334 and 347

48 Paul Bew (2007), *The Making and Remaking of the Good Friday Agreement,* op.cit., 61

49 Eamonn McCann (1999), *War and Peace in Northern Ireland,* Dublin: Hot Press Books, 236-7

50 Jonathan Powell, op.cit., 109

51 Eamonn McCann, Historical Handshakes do not reflect street-level reality, *Sunday Business Post,* 8 April 2007

52 Anthony McIntyre, We, the IRA, have failed, op.cit.

53 Party faithful look on Mallon as the heavyweight puncher who will leave political opponents bloodied, *Irish Times,* 2 April 1997 was the first time the expression was used

54 Gerry Adams (1986), *The Politics of Irish Freedom,* Dingle: Brandon, 110 for example

55 Austin Currie (2004), *All Hell Will Break Loose,* op.cit., 431-435

56 Irish Republican Army orders an end to armed campaign, *An Phoblacht-Republican News,* 28 July 2005

57 Jonathan Freedland, A nighmare ends, another nightmare begins, *The Guardian,* 29 July 2005

58 Ed Curran, Nelson Mandela 'was against IRA decommissioning', *Belfast Telegraph,* 2 July 2013

59 Anthony McIntyre, Another victory for unionism, *Sunday Tribune,* 4 July 1999

60 Ed Moloney (2007) *A Secret History of the IRA,* London: Allen Lane The Penguin Press, second and revised edition,

491-492

61   Ruairí Ó Brádaigh, When treason is not treason, *Fourthwrite*, Issue 8, 2001

62   Jim Cusack and Henry McDonald (2008), *UVF: The Endgame*, Dublin: Poolbeg, 429-431

63   General Sir Mike Jackson (2007), *Operation Banner: An Analysis of Military Operations in Northern Ireland prepared under the direction of the Chief of the General Staff.* Ministry of Defence: Army Code 71842, paragraph 855

64   Dan Keenan and Neil Carnduff, Intelligence forces recalled to North for security duty, *Irish Times*, 6 March 2009

65   Christopher Bass and M.L.R. Smith (2009), The war continues? Combating the paramilitaries and the role of the British Army after the Belfast Agreement, in: James Dingley (ed) *Combating Terrorism in Northern Ireland*, London: Routledge, 258

66   Jessie Blackbourn (2015), *Anti-Terrorism Law and Normalising Northern Ireland*, London: Routledge, 110, 115-116

67   Gerry Moriarty, PSNI recruitment shows difficulty of achieving uniform change in North, *Irish Times*, 12 January 2018

68   Cfr: Mary Gethins, *Catholic Police Officers in Northern Ireland: Voices Out of Silence*, Manchester: Manchester University Press, 2011

69   Paul Nolan (2012), *Northern Ireland Peace Monitoring Report Number One*, Belfast: Community Relations Council, 8 and 59

70   Jonathan Tonge (2006), *Northern Ireland*, Cambridge: Polity Press, 71

71   Paul Nolan (2014), *Northern Ireland Peace Monitoring Report Number Three*, Belfast: Community Relations Council, 45

72   Jessie Blackbourn (2015), op.cit., 183

73   Robin Wilson (2016), *Northern Ireland Peace Monitoring Report Number Four*, Belfast: Community Relations Council,

49

74 Daniel Holder (2013), Police accountability, the Irish peace process, and the continuing challenge of secrecy, *Race and Class*, 54: 3, 77-86

75 Adrian Rutherford and Deborah McAleese, Dissident Attacks prompt calls for special PSNI unit, *Belfast Telegraph*, 10 March 2010

76 Austen Morgan (2009), Northern Ireland Terrorism: The Legal Response, in: James Dingley (ed), *Combating Terrorism in Northern Ireland*, London: Routledge, 164

77 Jessie Blackbourn (2015), op.cit., 182

78 Robin Wilson (2016), op.cit., 43

79 Paul Nolan (2012), op.cit., 61-62

80 Gerry Moriarty, PSNI recruitment shows difficulty of achieving uniform change in North, op.cit.

81 That said, 187 of 228 IRA 'on the runs' benefited from, effectively, a secret UK Government amnesty concluded by Blair

82 Mark Simpson, Life as a protesting republican prisoner in Maghaberry, BBC website, 8 March 2012

83 Gerry Moriarty, Behind Maghaberry's walls: the prison left behind by peace, *Irish Times*, 25 March 2017

84 Omar Grech (2017), *Human Rights and the Northern Ireland Conflict: Law, Politics and Conflict*, 1921-2014, London: Routledge, chapter 7 passim

85 Conor Gearty, Brexit 2: why UK's Human Rights Act should not be repealed, *Irish Times*, 8 September 2016

86 Cfr. Duncan Campbell, Craigavon Two Suitable Scapegoats in wake of killing backlash, say supporters, *The Guardian*, 4 September 2013

87 Gerry Adams, Governments fail to honour obligations on crucial issues, *Belfast Telegraph*, 13 April 2013

88 Paul Bew and Henry Patterson (1985), *The British State and the Ulster Crisis*, London: Verso, 84

89   Paul Bew (2007), *Ireland: The Politics of Enmity 1789-2006*, op.cit., 549-550

90   Danny Morrison, A time to build trust, *The Observer*, 22 April 2001

91   Interview with Brendan Hughes, op.cit.

92   See for example the articles 'United We Stand' and 'Forward in Unity' in *An Phoblacht-Republican News*, 7 May 1998

93   Suzanne Breen, 'People did not die or take up arms for equality. They did so for Irish freedom', *Sunday Tribune*, 24 October 2010

94   Étienne Balibar (1998), *The Philosophy of Marx*, London: Verso, 89

95   Gerard Murray and Jonathan Tonge, op.cit., 261

96   Kevin Rafter (2005), *Sinn Féin 1905-2005: In the Shadow of Gunmen*, Dublin: Gill & Macmillan, 15, 138

97   In the same place, 242

98   Danny Morrison (1999), *Then The Walls Came Down: A Prison Journal*, Dublin and Cork: Mercier, 291

99   'Revolutionaries have to be pragmatic – wish lists are for Christmas', *An Phoblacht-Republican News*, 10 April 2008

100 Kevin Rafter, op.cit., 5

101 Danny Morrison, Paisley just a blip in the ongoing peace process, *Daily Ireland*, 9 February 2006

102 For more on this see: Georg Lukács (1972), *Tactics and Ethics 1919-1929: The Question of Parliamentarism and Other Essays*, London: NLB, 3-11

103 Edward W. Said (1995), *Peace & Its Discontents*, London: Vintage, 38

104 Joseph A. Massad (2006), *The Persistence of the Palestinian Question: Essays on Zionism and the Palestinians*, London: Routledge, 105

105 Edward W. Said, op.cit., xxix-xxx; Joseph A.Massad, op.cit.,113

106 Robbie McVeigh, Décolonisation inachevée en Irlande du

Nord, *Le Monde Diplomatique*, Avril 1999

107 Robbie McVeigh (2002), Bantustan Stormont and the Right of Self-Determination of the Irish People, in: Gerard McCann (ed) *The Rights Debate: sectoral opinions on human rights in the north of Ireland*, Belfast: West Belfast Economic Forum, 43-47

108 Joseph A. Massad, op.cit., 106

109 Martin Mansergh, The Future Path of Peace, *The Irish Reporter*, February 1996, 49

Part Three. 'Peace': What 'Dividends'?

It is frightfully hard to explain to Protestants that if you give Roman Catholics a good job and a good house they will live like Protestants.

Northern Ireland Unionist Prime Minister Terence O'Neill, Interview with *The Belfast Telegraph*, 10 May 1969

The worst about the Irish is that they become corruptible as soon as they stop being peasants and turn bourgeois. True, this is the case with most peasant nations. But in Ireland it is particularly bad. That is also why the press is so terribly lousy.

Friedrich Engels to Karl Marx, 27 September 1869

Peace dividends

Hope existed that the 1998 Agreement would be followed by 'peace dividends'. An important thing which is often forgotten is that the peace process is not just a political phenomenon, but also has an economic aspect. According to the government, 'peace process' plus neo-liberalism equals prosperity and will generate economic 'peace dividends'. This idea was developed as early as 1994 by the Confederation of British Industry[1]. The peace process goes hand in hand with the neo-liberal reconstruction of Northern Ireland. The photograph of former IRA commander and Sinn Féin leader Martin McGuinness with the pro-British unionist Ian Paisley opening the Nasdaq stock market in Wall Street on 5 December 2007 symbolises the idea that if the 'invisible hand' of the market gets its way, it will provide lasting peace and reconciliation. Economic development agencies from countries like Kosovo and Iraq have even been brought on official visits to the North to witness the success of that idea. If the peace process is sold abroad as a political model of conflict resolution, it is also appreciated as an economic model to emulate elsewhere[2]. What is happening in Northern Ireland is thus not simply a 'transition' from conflict to peace, but a transition towards a neo-liberal model of 'peace'[3].

Critics point out that this is fundamentally about transforming Northern Ireland into some kind of 'Potemkin Village' of neo-liberal peace to conceal the fact that it is a failed economic entity[4]. Because a detailed study of the evolution of the northern economy in the years since the Belfast Agreement seriously questions the degree to which the peace process has engendered a general and sustainable 'peace dividend', especially for the marginalised populations who suffered most during the conflict[5]. Even the chairman of the Confederation of British Industry has stated that despite the political peace dividend, there has been no real economic dividend and the North's economy has not moved on since 1998[6]. Her Majesty's Treasury provided this assessment in a paper published in 2011: 'Peace has not in itself been sufficient to raise Northern Ireland prosperity to the UK average or even to the UK average excluding South East England. Northern Ireland still has one of the weakest economies in the UK[7].'

Failed economic entity

However, the peace process and neo-liberalism have not altered the fact that Northern Ireland remains a failed economic entity. The region is dependent upon British financial subsidies. The British government spends £5850 per year for every person living in Northern Ireland. Northern Ireland's fiscal deficit is 38.3 per cent of its gross domestic product (GDP), whereas the UK average is 12 per cent. To take an international example, Greece's fiscal deficit stood at 13.6 per cent of its GDP in 2010 whereas in Northern Ireland it stood at 32 per cent that year.

Economically, Northern Ireland is characterised by:

Low productivity – it is 85 per cent of the UK average and the third lowest of all UK regions (in terms of gross value added per employee); it is only 60 per cent of the Republic of Ireland figure.

Low wages – the 2015 ratio stands at 92 per cent of the UK average and is the lowest of all UK regions.

Much higher level of economic inactivity – 26.0 per cent of the working-age population in the first quarter of 2016, the highest as ever of the 12 UK regions, as against 21.8 per cent for the UK as a whole. This has left the *employment* rate in Northern Ireland at 69.6 per cent, nearly 5 percentage points short of that across the UK, 74.2 per cent.

Living standards below UK average – public spending represents over 70 per cent of Northern Ireland's GDP – OECD countries average is about 28 per cent. Over 30 per cent of the workforce directly works for the public sector. Northern Ireland is the only place in the UK where wages are higher than they are in the private sector – public sector wages are on average 41.5 per cent higher than those in the private sector; and private-sector wages are the lowest of the UK, 82.8 per cent of the UK average[8]. In absolute terms private-sector weekly incomes are still much lower (£429) than public (£577).

From all the above, it is evident that Northern Ireland is not a success in terms of economic development. Its economy 'remains on a path characterised by low investment, low productivity, low employment and low incomes[9]'. The low investment rate in Northern Ireland has been translated into a steady fall in labour productivity, measured as output per person employed, relative to the UK average. Between 2000 and 2014, the North's productivity fell from 93 per cent of the UK average to 80 per cent[10]. So much for Northern Ireland PLC! Having reached a peak of 88.2 per cent of the UK average in 2007, Northern Ireland's gross disposable household income per head fell to 81.5 per cent of the mean in 2014, the last year for which data from the Office for National Statistics are available. Contrary to widespread expectations of a 'peace dividend' specific to the region, in 2014 gross disposable household income in Northern Ireland was exactly the same proportion of the UK figure as in the last pre-Agreement year, 1997. And Households Below Average Income data show that median household income in 2014-15 was, at £380 per week after housing costs, almost identical in real terms to a decade earlier[11].

Living conditions

The people who were the most affected by the conflict are those who benefit the least from 'peace dividends'. In a 2011 report, the Northern Ireland Assembly's Research and Library Service studied deprivation and social disadvantage since 1998. It found little evidence of 'peace dividend' and that the gap between the well-off and the disadvantaged had persisted and in some cases increased since the signing of the Good Friday Agreement. Of the 56 wards ranked as the most deprived 10 per cent in 2001, the researchers found that only 14 areas had climbed out of deprivation by 2010. In some cases this had been achieved only because of boundary changes[12].

These conclusions were further confirmed by a study published in 2016 on social and economic conditions since 1994 in the 36 Neighbourhood Renewal Areas in the North most affected by the conflict. Based on official social and economic indicators for eduction, employment, economic inactivity, mental health and suicide, life expectancy, and health and criminality, the study concludes that those areas did not benefit from 'peace divideds' in terms of income, employment or quality of life since the 1994 ceasefires and that in many cases conditions had worsened[13]. Another academic study also published in 2016 shows that current austerity measures such as the 2012 Welfare Reform Act will significantly worsen the living conditions of those who have been most affected by the conflict[14].

The problem of suicide is particularly serious. The British

Prime Minister claims that Northern Ireland is the happiest region in the UK[15]. But statistics give clear indications that mental health problems increased during the peace period. Studies show that the suicide rate in Northern Ireland has grown from 8.6 per 100,000 in 1998 to 16 per 100,000 in 2008[16]. From 1970 to 2015, 7697 suicides were recorded in Northern Ireland, and 318 suicides in 2015 represents the highest amount since 1970[17].

For all these reasons, Northern Ireland's main daily newspaper was right to conclude in 2013 that 15 years after the 1998 Agreement there is a deficit of peace dividends[18]. The Northern Irish example shows that the economic aspect of the peace process is unable to either generate economic prosperity or lasting 'peace dividends' for the people who were most affected by the conflict and has seen a growing increase of social and economic inequalities[19].

Nationalists 'part of the establishment as never before'

The Belfast Agreement has a double logic. On the one hand, it represents a defeat for republicanism, copper fastens partition and strengthens British rule. But on the other hand, it also represents a victory for nationalism in that it advances nationalist communal interests within the North itself. As Suzanne Breen points out: 'There has been undeniable advancement in many areas for Catholics in the North, but within existing constitutional arrangements[20].' This to a large extent explains why the majority of Nationalists in the North see the peace process as a step forward.

Research carried out 10 years after the 1998 Agreement by academics from Queen's University showed that Catholics gained more from the social and economic benefits of the peace process than Protestants and concluded that it is the nationalist community which is making the most of the opportunities in the post-Troubles era[21]. It is thus not surprising that the Sinn

Féin newspaper could note in 1994 'the tide of history with nationalists' and in 1998 the 'growing confidence within the nationalist community[22]'. Broadly speaking, the nationalist population has seen substantial improvement in its material conditions, and has a feeling of being dynamic and on the move. One of the most striking facts is that the average hourly wage for nationalists and republicans (£9.44 per hour) is now higher than that of pro-British unionists (£9.11 per hour)[23]. Nationalists are today much more comfortable with and less alienated from state institutions in Northern Ireland. Second-class citizens for a long time and an 'oppressed minority', nationalists have now become 'equals'[24].

In January 2018 the Executive Office published its latest Labour Force Survey Religion Report covering the years 1992 to 2016. This report proves this trend. In 1992, 76 per cent of working-age Protestants were economically active, compared with 66 per cent of working-age Catholics. By 2016, these figures had fallen to 75 per cent for Protestants, but risen to 74 per cent for Catholics. In 1992, 24 per cent of working-age Protestants were economically inactive compared with 34 per cent of working-age Catholics, a 10 percentage point difference. In 2016, the rates were 25 per cent for Protestants and 26 per cent for Catholics. Over the period 1993 to 2016, the proportion of working-age economically active Protestants with no qualifications fell from 30 per cent to 11 per cent, but the numbers of Catholics without skills fell by slightly more, from 32 per cent to 10 per cent[25].

A central idea in left-wing and republican discourse during the 1970s and 1980s was that Northern Ireland was 'irreformable' – it was impossible for nationalists to gain civil rights or equality within Northern Ireland. However, the effects and reforms and positive discrimination by the British state shows that this conclusion was wrong or at least premature.

In 1975, the Canadian scholar E.A. Aunger carried out the most in-depth study concerning the relation between religion, social class and work. This study based mainly on the 1971 census showed that Catholics were under-represented in the most prestigious jobs and highest positions but were over-represented in the lower social categories and occupations[26]. However, the impact of direct rule, reforms and the expansion of the public sector (a sort of 'counter-insurgency Keynesianism') have resulted in very significant upward social mobility for the nationalist population. By the 1990s, nationalists were very much present among accountants, professionals, banking, architects, university jobs and the public sector[27]. If in 1971, only 15 per cent of engineers and 18 per cent of accountants came from the nationalist community, by 1991 it was respectively 31 per cent and 42 per cent[28].

The traditional nationalist middle-class in Northern Ireland was made up mostly of teachers, lawyers, priests, doctors and pub owners and was essentially orientated towards the Catholic population. In contrast, the new Catholic middle-class is essentially concentrated in the public sector and is gradually rising to its top. This has been confirmed by a study based on the results of the 1971, 1981 and 1991 census[29].This nationalist middle-class is also called 'new' as its arrival in that social category is quite recent. A study based on the 2001 census indicates that only 17 per cent of Catholics belonging to the highest social and economic category were born in it compared to 33 per cent of protestants[30].

If on the basis of the 2011 census Catholics in Northern Ireland still have a higher unemployment rate (9 per cent compared to 6 per cent for Protestants), have more health problems (11 per cent compared to 8 per cent for Protestants), live in overcrowded accomodation (12 per cent compared to 6 per cent for Protestants), this has to be nuanced by the fact that they have experienced an unprecedented social mobility. If in 2001, two out of the 20 most affluent areas in the North had a nationalist majority compared to 16 of the 20 most socially and economically deprived, by 2011 nationalists now dominated six of the 20 most affluent wards[31].

From a social and economic point of view, the new Catholic middle-class clearly appears as the winner of the peace process. As Paul Bew noted, this has led to a shift in the nationalist population from a mood of 'rage' to one of 'vanity'[32] and the development of a kind of kulak mentality. The richest part of Belfast, the Malone Road, now has a nationalist majority, and the majority of customers for private jets came from that community, which made one commentator pertinently ask: 'What did Bobby Sands kill himself for anyway? Was it so that his fellow northern Catholics could own jets? Drive BMWs[33]?'

A 'cold house for Protestants'?

On the question of the consitutional position of Northern Ireland, the peace process has reinforced the Union with the United Kingdom. Unionist First Minister and DUP leader Arlene Foster said in 2016 that she was absolutely certain the constitutional status was secure and claimed the Union was stronger[34]. The fact that the Union is secure is reinforced by the fact that in her first speech as Prime Minister, Theresa May stated: 'Not everybody knows this, but the full title of my party is the Conservative and Unionist Party and that word unionist is very important to me[35].' On 26 June 2017 a DUP confidence-and-supply support for a Conservative minority government led by Theresa May was secured.

But what is paradoxal is that if the peace process represents a victory for unionism, many Protestants feel they are on the losing side[36]. As Eamonn McCann notes: 'the Protestant working class, and its young people in particular, have been the main losers from change in Northern Ireland...They feel – and it's a feeling they know is endorsed and welcomed by many nationalists – that Catholics are on the way up, Protestants on the way down[37].' One just has to look at the fact that while universities and institutions of higher education now have a republican and nationalist majority, 13 out of the 15 areas with the worst academic and school results are in pro-British unionist areas. It is estimated that a person coming from a poor republican or nationalist background will have one chance out of five to go to university whereas someone from a poor unionist background one chance out of ten[38]. Today 24 per cent of Protestants in the 16 to 24 years age group are unemployed compared to 17 per cent for Catholics[39]. Traditional sources of employment of the pro-British population such as shipbuilding also evaporated due to de-industrialisation and other tendencies. So they have the feeling of having lost, whereas the nationalist population's quality of life gets better which makes them think they have won. Back in 2001, the then British Secretary of State for Northern Ireland noted that 'today, Catholics are part of the establishment as never before' but underlined 'Protestant alienation' and warned of the danger that Northern Ireland could become a 'cold house for protestants[40]'.

The paradox is that nationalists and republicans seem on the rise while they lost the constitutional dispute while Unionists and Loyalists feel they have lost while the Union has been copper-fastened. Indeed, on 25 June 1999, British Prime Minister Tony Blair noted that pro-British unionists 'are too stupid to realise that they have won and Sinn Féin too clever to admit they have lost[41]'. The Unionist First Minister of Northern Ireland and leader of the Democratic and Unionist Party also stated in 2014 that: 'Unionists are capable of extracting defeat from the jaws of victory and nationalists and republicans are capable of gaining victory from the jaws of defeat[42].' This feeling of defeat pushes unionists to the right, blaming immigrants and Catholics for their decline.

Privatised peace

Power-sharing institutions in Northern Ireland functioned only from 2 December 1999 to 11 February 2000, and from 30 May

2000 to 14 October 2002. They were suspended by the British government for the rest of the time, proving that it is in London that effective sovereigny lies. During that time, British and Irish governments organised negotiations between the Northern Irish political parties to re-establish power-sharing and implement the totality of the 1998 Agreement. These new negotiations were centred upon Sinn Féin and the Democratic Unionist Party which had become the largest political parties in Northern Ireland following their success in various elections between 2001 and 2005. The decline of the UUP and the SDLP since the first Assembly election of 25 June 1998 has been dramatic. In 1998, the SDLP gained the highest number of first-preference votes (177,963) and 24 seats, whereas it won 12 seats in the 2 March 2017 Northern Ireland Assembly Elections and attracted 95,958 votes. It is the same story for the UUP. At the first Assembly election it won 28 seats and 172,225 first-preference votes, compared with 10 seats and 103,314 votes in 2017. In contrast, the DUP went from 145,917 votes and 24 seats in 1998 to 225,413 votes and 28 seats in 2017; while Sinn Féin gained 142,858 votes and 17 seats in 1998 the party received 224,245 votes and 27 seats in 2017. While after the 1997 general elections, out of the 18 Northern Ireland seats in Westminster the UUP had 10 MPs, the SDLP 3, and DUP and Sinn Féin 2 each, both the UUP and the SDLP lost their representation at Westminster after the 8 June 2017 with the DUP controlling 10 seats and Sinn Féin 7. Between 1998 and 2017 the UUP vote fell by 40 per cent, the SDLP vote fell by 46 per cent, while the DUP vote grew by 54.5 per cent and the Sinn Féin vote grew almost 57 per cent. It would be wrong to see in Sinn Féin and the DUP's electoral success the triumph of 'extremes' over 'moderates' and the radicalisation of the electorate. What happened rather was a 'moderation of extremes' – Sinn Féin and the DUP adopted the positions of their 'moderate' rivals and now occupy the centre ground[43]. According to Tony Catney, the party's former head of electoral strategy, Sinn Féin attracts 'new Catholic money...

largely apolitical but nationalistic in its aspirations[44]'. Sinn Féin and the DUP can be characterised as 'ethnic tribune' parties that 'seek to maximise the group's share of resources extractable from participation in the power-sharing institutions. The ethnic tribune party can be simultaneously pragmatic over resources and intransigent about identity[45].' The politics of the Northern Ireland Assembly function on the basis of a system of 'ethnic outbidding' where the strongest voice advocating respective ethnic group interests has the upper hand[46].

The outcome of those negotiations was the St Andrews Agreement on 13 October 2006. According to a DUP document, the St Andrews Agreement made fundamental changes to the 1998 Agreement and offered from a unionist perspective 'undoubtedly a better package' compared to its predecessor. It offers unionists a strengthened veto over Sinn Féin. According to leading constitutional expert Rick Wilford, Professor of Politics at QUB, changes made at St Andrews mean that unionists are able to torpedo policies they don't like, such as attempts to strengthen North-South institutions or an Irish Language Act[47]. On 26 March 2007 the DUP and Sinn Féin finally agreed to share power from 8 May onwards. This was welcomed by the media, but some observers compared it to a 'Hitler-Stalin pact Ulster style' rather than a model for world peace[48].

From 8 May 2007 to 9 January 2017 the DUP and Sinn Féin shared power without interruption. The Republican Movement that Ian Paisley went into government with is not the Republican Movement that was resisting unionist rule and trying to overthrow the British for the best part of 3 or 4 decades. Like what Edward W. Said had said about the PLO, Sinn Féin 'has transformed itself from a liberation movement into a kind of small-town government[49]'. Under the 'new dispensation', governance structures have been assembled to reconfigure post-conflict economic space. 'The onset of devolution has promoted a mix between ethno-sectarian resource competition and a constantly expanding neoliberal model of governance.' All governing parties subscribe to the virtues of free market enterprise, austerity finance, urban regeneration, public-private partnership, private-finance initiatives and foreign direct investment by global multinationals. Neo-liberal principles of privatisation, fiscal conservatism and low social welfare are seen as the main engines of social and economic peace dividend[50]. Peace has in effect been 'privatised'.

A detailed examination of the Northern Ireland Assembly's policies in terms of welfare reform, education of childcare benefits shows that they reinforce social and economic inequality[51]. This neo-liberal consensus between the ruling parties is reinforced by the fact that the Assembly has very limited powers, is compelled to apply directives coming from London and has no say in terms of taxation for instance. There is a consensus among the parties in the Assembly that the solution to Northern Ireland's economic problems should be based on cutting corporation tax rates.

On 23 December 2014, Northern Irish political parties finalised the Stormont House Agreement, where in exchange for London promising the Assembly the right to cut corporation tax rates in a few years time, Sinn Féin and the DUP engaged themselves to cut 20,000 jobs in the public sector, to cut welfare benefits and accept a reduction of £200 million per year in money coming from London[52]. These measures became concrete on 17 November 2015 in *A Fresh Start: the Stormont Agreement and Implementation Plan* agreed by the Assembly. Power-sharing collapsed when Martin McGuinness resigned on 9 January 2017 as Northern Ireland's Deputy First Minister in protest against the handling of a botched energy scheme (Renewable Heating Initiative, colloquially known as 'Cash for Ash') that could cost taxpayers £490m. At the time of writing negotiations are still ongoing in order to resurrect the local Assembly.

A benign form of apartheid?

For many observers, 'peace' today in Northern Ireland can at best be described as a 'benign form of apartheid'. Segregation and divisions have significantly increased since 1998[53]. Neoliberal peace failed to normalise the six counties. Twenty years after the 1998 Agreement, Northern Ireland remains a highly divided society. Various indicators show that in many areas divisions in terms of housing and school segregation have actually increased[54]. This is more a case of 'reconciliation under duress' to borrow T.W. Adorno's expression than a lasting peace. Walls dividing Catholic from Protestant areas have risen from 22 at the time of the 1998 Agreement to 88 today. Those barriers testify to the political failure to bring a lasting peace[55]. With its failure to bring peace dividend or develop reconciliation, the 're-branding' of the six counties is a case of 'putting lipstick on a gorilla[56]'. The peace process has thus not allowed reconcliation between the adversaries but has intensified their divisions and institutionalised them.

The growth of these divisions is related to the fact that with the peace process, the conflict has been fundamentally re-defined. Previously, the conflict was clearly understood as a political conflict between two opposite political ideologies – republicanism and unionism, the question was who was ultimately sovereign, the British state or the people of Ireland as a whole. The peace process has fundamentally altered this: the conflict is now re-defined not as a political dispute between two opposite political ideologies, but as a cultural clash between two different cultural identities[57]. According to this new paradigm, the reason why there has been a conflict in Northern Ireland is because the Irish cultural identity was not respected and people thought the British cultural identity was under threat. The solution is to show 'parity of esteem' and respect to all identities and cultures. However, the parameters of the conflict between republicanism and unionism were not about

British identity versus Irish identity, but between Thomas Paine and Edmund Burke[58]. It is also interesting to note that when unionism developed over 100 years ago, its architects considered themselves to be Irish unionists and not on the basis of a British cultural identity[59].

From irreconcilable political projects, republicanism and unionism have now been transformed into different 'traditions' between which there should be 'equality' and 'parity of esteem'. This has been facilitated by Section 75 of the Northern Ireland Act 1998, which defends this equality legally, and the Equality Commission set up on 1 October 1999. For Gerry Adams, the 1998 Agreement 'secured remarkable progress' as 'equality lies at its core[60]'. However, this is 'equality between communities, parity of esteem between traditions, rather than any universalist conception of egalitarianism in terms of outcomes. There is a substantive difference between parity of esteem for divergent cultures and greater material equality based on communautarian principles[61].' Consequently, the concept of equality is emptied of its content. The actors of the conflict have ceased to formulate their demands in terms of universalist principles but in terms of particularist demands of parity between communal identities. The peace process is not about conflict resolution or conflict transformation but rather about 'conflict management' of 'different identities'.

All the ruling parties now accept the legitimacy of British rule and of neo-liberal policies, so they now have to differ mainly on symbolic issues such as flags, an Irish Language Act etc and to lobby the state to ensure 'parity of esteem' on these issues[62]. Republicanism was never about particularistic ethnic demands but universalistic claims, so the new politics of Sinn Féin are essentially a form of identity politics[63]. In the case of an Irish Language Act, it is interesting that The Economist notes: 'More important, Irish gives Sinn Féin a popular issue to cover its climbdown from traditional demands for Irish unity[64].' But in terms of the Irish language, the priority of republicans should lie elsewhere. As Gilles Deleuze puts it:

> We must be bilingual even in a single language, we must have a minor language inside our own language, we must create a minor use of our own language. Multilingualism is not merely the property of several systems each of which would be homogeneous in itself: it is primarily the line of flight or a variation which affects each system by stopping it of being homogeneous. Not speaking like an Irish person...in a language other than one's own, but on the contrary speaking in one's language like a foreigner[65].

The result of all this is that Northern Ireland has gone from the politics of imperialism versus anti-imperialism to the narcissism of small differences[66]. From an enlightened point of view as Edward W. Said puts it: 'There's so much factionalism, so much sectarianism, so much petty squabbling over definitions and identities that people have lost sight of the important goal, as Aimé Césaire described it, the rendezvous of victory, where all peoples in search of freedom and emancipation and enlightenment gather[67].'

The transformation of political aspirations into cultural ones goes hand in hand with greater emphasis being given to the symbolic rather than the material.

> It's because some Nationalists are uneasy at their own acceptance of Northern Ireland that they feel they have to make a show of rhetorical opposition to it. It is because, in practical terms, they have endorsed the legitimacy of the Northern Ireland State that they denounce symbolic representations of it all the more loudly. The campaign to obliterate Northern Ireland having halted, they turn to battle on who'll rule the roost within it[68].

The dispute over the flying of the Union Jack in Belfast City Hall illustrates all those tendencies. On 3 December 2012, Sinn Féin councillors in Belfast City Council voted in favour of a motion for the Union Jack to be flown only 18 days out of 365 as in the rest of the UK rather than the entire year. The party argued that to have the flag out the entire year showed a lack of respect to those claiming an Irish identity, but unionists claimed that to bring down the flag showed they were losing their British identity. However, as Jason Walsh argues:

A properly republican response to British sovereignty in Northern Ireland would not be to dispute the fact of its existence by lowering flags, but rather to question it and argue for Irish sovereignty. Alas, the...motion...focused on the cultural trappings of sovereignty – identity – rather than its reality. Likewise, the Loyalist response ignores actual reality: power-sharing has strengthened British rule in Ireland...Instead, Loyalists have chosen to focus on shrill and shallow 'union jackery'...Unfortunately, virtually the only answers on offer, from politicians and commentators alike, is yet more peace process: more cultural recognition, more identity politics and more demands for respect. The poison of identity politics is that in seeking to channel political demands, whether for a united Ireland or the United Kingdom, into questions of culture, the peace process does the opposite of settling the dispute: it permanently enshrines it and keeps Unionists and republicans locked together in a proxy conflict[69].

Victims industry and therapy culture

The peace process has put significant emphasis on the 'victims' of the conflict. The 1998 Belfast Agreement stated: 'The tragedies of the past have left a deep and profoundly regrettable legacy of suffering. We must never forget those who have died or been injured, and their families.' From Kenneth Bloomfield's report published shortly after on 29 April 1998 to the Eames-Bradley proposals made public on 28 January 2009 and the recent 'Fresh Start' agreement, 'victims' have been at the centre of Northern Ireland's political discourse. A search made in 2013 in the archives section of the online version of the Belfast Telegraph brought up more than 9000 articles on the 'victims' of the conflict from the 1990s onwards. According to the Northern Ireland Commission for Victims and Survivors, from 1998 to 2010 over £80 million has been invested in developing the Northern Ireland victims sector. By 2014 there were almost 50 dedicated victim and survivor groups in operation in Northern Ireland, rising to 90 when 'parallel providers' (who do not work only with conflict-related victims) are included. Indeed obviously sympathetic commentators, such as Sir Kenneth Bloomfield (himself the victim of an IRA bomb), have bemoaned the development of a 'victims industry'[70] in Northern Ireland.

This 'victims industry' is closely connected to a 'victim culture'. People are fighting to be recognised as being 'more' of a victim or a more 'deserving' victim than others. There is no agreed definition of what a 'victim' of the conflict is or who can fit into that category. But as the Lacanian psychoanalyst Jacqueline Rose noted: 'Victimhood is an event. It is something that happens to you. The moment it becomes an identity, psychological or political, then I think you're finished[71].' From active subject, people define themselves as victim instead. The Bloody Sunday March for Justice in January 2018 was subject to a huge controversy because the poster advertising it included references not only to the 14 civilians shot dead by the Parachute Regiment in January 1972, but also to British soldiers killed by republicans, IRA massacres such as Omagh, Shankill and Kingsmill and even the 2017 Grenfell Tower disaster. What unites all these disparate events is the sense of victimhood. Everybody is a victim of some sort. The central importance given to this 'victim' discourse is symptomatic not only of the crisis of republicanism and unionism, but of a general weakened sense of agency.

The problem of 'victims' raises that of 'therapy culture'. Most studies in the existing literature stress that the population of the six counties has been heavily traumatised by the conflict there. A study providing epidemiological estimates of trauma, post-traumatic stress disorder and associated mental disorders in Northern Ireland, with a focus on the impact of the conflict using data from the NI Study of Health and Stress as well as a representative epidemiological survey of adults in the region, estimated that 60.6 per cent of people there had a lifetime traumatic event, and 39.0 per cent experienced a presumed conflict-related event[72]. Another report on the trans-generational impact of the conflict also found that more than 213,000 people in Northern Ireland are experiencing significant mental health problems as a result of the conflict[73]. The existence of such 'trauma' brings the issue of 'healing' and how people affected can move forward.

The problem with current approaches is that they understand 'trauma' as essentially a medical and mental health issue and medicalise 'healing'. They reduce what is a political problem to a therapeutic one. This introspective, individualised and depoliticised approach promotes a view of the human subject as inherently vulnerable and in need of professional support (a perspective similar to 'victim culture'), what Frank Furedi has called 'therapy culture'. Furedi interestingly points to evidence for this new therapeutic sensibility in the increase in citations of the words 'stress', 'syndrome', 'counselling' and 'trauma' (the latter increased tenfold from less than 500 mentions to over 5000) in British newspapers between 1994 and 2000. The start date is significant as 1994 is the year of the ceasefires that marked the public phase of the peace process[74]. However one should bear in mind that 'healing' is only one means of dealing with the legacy of violent conflict, and one that is not necessarily favoured by those who have been affected by the Troubles. The Report of the Victims Commissioner, for example, noted that groups representing those who had been killed directly by state forces, or killed in instances allegedly involving state collusion between the state and Loyalist death squads, expressed a firm view that revelation of the full truth of these controversial events was far more important for the victims they represented than any other consideration. The relatives who are searching for 'truth' frame the issue of dealing with the past in terms of 'justice' rather than in terms of 'healing'. Healing, if it is considered at all, is viewed as a secondary issue and one that will be an outcome of achieving justice. When we talk about 'healing' war-torn societies we should recognise that healing is not a discrete process that only takes place in a therapeutic setting; it is tied up with wider questions of social justice and normative concerns about what type of society we all want to inhabit. Ultimately, these wider issues can only be addressed in the political domain[75].

But a major obstacle to those wider issues being properly addressed in the political domain is that some of the approaches to dealing with the past tend to reduce history to psychodrama. The best example of this was the Facing The Truth programmes broadcast by the BBC in March 2006 in which Desmond Tutu brought people who had lost relatives in the conflict together with the person responsible for their loss in the hope of encouraging them to make gestures of forgiveness and reconciliation in front of the cameras. This became in effect a denial of a political approach to dealing with a past that looked beyond interpersonal encounters to the structural causes of conflict and violence[76]. In his essay On Cosmopolitanism and Forgiveness, Jacques Derrida shows the difficulties associated with the concepts of 'forgiveness' and 'reconciliation' and the tensions that can arise between the two. Using the South African Truth Commission of Desmond Tutu as an example, Derrida argues that the concept of 'forgiveness' is misplaced when used in relation to a national trauma. There are tensions between individual 'forgiveness' and national 'reconciliation', and the state could avoid being held accountable if everything was simply a matter of individual 'forgiveness'. 'Forgiveness' and 'reconciliation' are therefore not synonymous and can fall short of 'justice'.[77]

This last point is particularly relevant if one looks at official 'apologies' given by the British state for some of its actions during the conflict in the North. A recent study critically examining the nature, role and function of official apologies with respect to conflict-related deaths in Northern Ireland concludes by suggesting that a pattern of official apologies without accountability and acceptance of responsibility is emerging in Northern Ireland; that official apologies can function as a way to shield state institutions, deflect further scrutiny, deny culpability, avoid effective redress and placate and silence victims. In this context historical injustice may be intensified rather than rectified, causing more harm than good, at best glossing over past wrongs and at worst facilitating impunity and re-traumatising victims[78]. The paradox is that the very need to apologise for some of its actions during the conflict represents an attempt to justify them which can only increase the guilt of the British state. What Paul de Man wrote in a famous passage of Allegories of Reading is directly relevant to the British state's apologies: 'Excuses not only accuse but they carry out the verdict implicit in their accusation...Excuses generate the very guilt they exonerate, though always in excess or by default...No excuse can ever hope to catch up with such a proliferation of guilt[79].'

Inquiries, 'legacy issues' and the past

The issue of official 'apologies' arose in the context of the many official enquiries that have taken place since 1998: more than £500 million has been spent by the British government (and to a lesser extent by Leinster House) for inquiries into some controversal incidents of the conflict[80]. The most important of those inquiries has been the Saville Inquiry. On 29 January 1998 British Prime Minister Tony Blair promised an official inquiry into Bloody Sunday, and on 15 June 2010 the Saville Inquiry made its conclusions public. The Saville Inquiry into Bloody Sunday lasted 12 years and cost £195 million, making it the longest and most expensive public inquiry in UK history. In comparison the official inquiry into the 9/11 attack in the USA in which 2995 people lost their lives lasted for 20 months, interviewed more than 1200 witnesses in ten countries, reviewed more than 2.5 million pages of documentation and cost $15 million. The Saville Inquiry shows how 'inquiry culture' connects with both therapy and victim culture and provides new means for the British state to reassert its authority in the six counties. As Brendan O'Neill put it:

> The impact of the rewriting of the Bloody Sunday story by the modern British state has been twofold: first, it has helped to dehistoricise that day; and second, it has helped turn it into a vehicle for therapeutic intervention into the lives of people in Northern Ireland, who apparently require a new army of British-funded experts to help them come to terms with their tragic pasts...Indeed, so thorough has been the lawyerly makeover of Bloody Sunday that the British state, the author of the atrocity, can now assume its moral authority in Ireland through taking an apologetic approach to such tragic historic events. In scolding some of its soldiers and offering apologies to their victims, the British state has extricated itself from the history and politics of Bloody Sunday, taking the elevated position of a dispassionate fixer of past wrongs. Today, one of the key ways Britain justifies its continuing presence in Ireland is as a moral manager of the past, a facilitator of reconciliation between hurting communities – and its moral hijacking of Bloody Sunday has been a key plank in this

rehabilitation of its rule in a neighbouring nation...Bloody Sunday was not a freak incident in which paras 'lost control' – it was part of a war by the British state to maintain control over its colony of Northern Ireland. And now, 40 years on, that same tragic event is used by the same British state to reassert, in therapeutic terms, its governance of Northern Ireland[81].

The Stormont House Agreement of 23 December 2014 promised another £150 million to be spent over the following 5 years to deal with the 'past' and so-called 'legacy issues' about which there is no consensus. From the previous inquiries it is possible to have an idea about how the debate about the past is going to be framed:

> The end result is a shallow debate about the past, where questions about who was fundamentally responsible for the conflict are evaded, and an uncritical approach in the present, where the authority of the British state in Northern Ireland is judged by the gestures it makes to the 'hurting' communities rather than by its policies or vision or, indeed, its legitimacy[82].

The fact that it is the British state which determines the parameters on how to deal with the past has the following implication: 'They suggest that we start the exploration of the past on the understanding that the laws of the State decide who was in the right and who in the wrong through a conflict over the very legitimacy of that State[83].' The result of this is that in Northern Ireland not every murder will be treated the same:

> Everyone in the UK has heard of Jean McConville. She was a mother of ten, abducted and murdered by the Provisional IRA in 1972 (accused of being an informer). It is a case used to highlight the inhumanity of the IRA. But who is Joan Connolly?

She was a mother of eight shot by the Parachute Regiment in the unprovoked killing of 11 civilians in Ballymurphy in West Belfast in 1971. The Secretary of State for Northern Ireland has refused an enquiry into these murders. Justice for these two mothers is not equal[84].

In May 2018 Theresa May, and before her the Northern Ireland Secretary of State as well as other Conservative and Unionist elements, complained that there was a 'disproportionate focus' on the state in terms of 'legacy issues' and even claimed that former soldiers who served in Northern Ireland were now victims of a 'witch hunt'. However, of the conflict deaths being investigated in 2018 just 28.5 per cent are attributed to the security forces. Based on the figures released by the DPP from 2011 to 2017, prosecutors in Northern Ireland have pursued five times more prosecutions against alleged paramilitaries than against soldiers[85]. This is a direct consequence of the fact that: 'For the state, the monopoly of legitimate force that has been re-established as a result of the peace process must logically encompass the monopoly of determining what force is legitimate[86].' How to deal with the 'past' is made on terms ultimately dictated by the British state and is not built on justice or truth.

Conclusion

There are solid reasons to doubt that social and economic prosperity will be generated by associating peace process and neo-liberalism. On the contrary, as this chapter demonstrates, neo-liberalism has failed to produce 'peace dividends' for those who have been most affected by the conflict, and divisions have increased. The Northern Ireland case is not unique. A study comparing the 'double transition' (towards a 'post-conflict' society and a 'neo-liberal' society) in Northern Ireland, South Africa and Poland demonstrates that in these three cases it failed to generate lasting 'dividends' for those most affected by this transition and has witnessed growing social and economic inequality[87].

In this 'Potemkin Village' of neo-liberal peace that is Northern Ireland, therapy culture, victims industry, the narcissism of small differences and the sentimentalisation of public life indicate a weakened sense of agency, the collapse of historical forces, diminished political expectations and a new way for the British state to reassert its authority in the six counties. The current victim, therapy and inquiry culture enables the British state to reassert, in therapeutic terms, its governance of Northern Ireland. But it also stresses the alarming extent to which since 1998 in Northern Ireland therapeutic politics have usurped politics proper. As Chris Gilligan concluded in his study of conflict-related trauma policy in Northern Ireland: 'In order to rebuild a society torn by conflict a more ambitious and active vision is needed, one which looks to the future and what people can do to bring about this future.'

Endnotes

1   Cfr: Confederation of British Industry Northern Ireland, (1994), *Peace – A Challenging New Era*, Belfast: CBINI

2   See for example: Portland Trust (2007), *Economics in Peacemaking: Lessons from Northern Ireland*, London: The Portland Trust

3   Dr Conor McCabe (2013), *The Double Transition: The Economic and Political Transition of Peace*, Dublin: Irish Congress of Trade Unions, 3 and 19. See also: David Cannon (2011) *Northern Ireland and the political economy of peace: neo-liberalism and the end of the Troubles*, PhD thesis, School of History and Politics, University of Adelaide

4   John Nagle (2009), Potemkin Village: Neo-liberalism and Peace-building in Northern Ireland? *Ethnopolitics: Formerly*

Global Review of Ethnopolitics, 8:2, 187

5   Denis O'Hearn (2008), How has Peace Changed the Northern Irish Political Economy? *Ethnopolitics: Formerly Global Review of Ethnopolitics*, 7:1, 101-118

6   Francess McDonnell, Sectarianism in workplace dampens jubilee cheer, *Irish Times*, 22 May 2012

7   HM Treasury (2011), *Rebalancing the Northern Ireland Economy*, London: HM Treasury, 3

8   Paul Nolan (2013), *Northern Ireland Peace Monitoring Report Number Two*, Belfast: Community Relations Council, 20, 26-27; Paul Nolan (2014), op.cit., 20-21 and Robin Wilson (2016), op.cit., 76, 90 for all these figures

9   Robin Wilson (2016), op.cit., 17

10   John FitzGerald: North remains land of lost opportunities, *Irish Times*, 26 October 2017

11   Robin Wilson (2016), op.cit., 19

12   Diana Rusk, Quality of life in north's deprived areas worsens, *Irish News*, 24 March 2011. This paper prepared by the Northern Ireland Assembly, Research and Library Service (B. Love (2011), *Deprivation and social disadvantage in Northern Ireland 1998-2010*, NIAR 133-11, Belfast: Northern Ireland Assembly, Research and Library Service) which tracked some of these indicators has been withdrawn from the official website. As Colin Knox pointed out, could politicians or officials be fearful of what these data would reveal and their political sensitivity?

13   Colin Knox (2016), Northern Ireland: where is the peace dividend?, *Policy & Politics*, 44:3, 485-503

14   Mike Tomlinson (2016) Risking peace in the 'war against the poor'? Social exclusion and the legacies of the Northern Ireland conflict, *Critical Social Policy*, 36:1, 104-123

15   Ellen Branagh, Northern Ireland people labelled happiest in the UK, *Belfast Telegraph*, 29 February 2012

16   Michael W Tomlinson (2012). War, peace and suicide: The

case of Northern Ireland, *International Sociology*, 27:4, 464-482

17   Kathryn Torney, Suicide deaths in North hit 318 – the highest on record, *Irish Times*, 29 July 2016

18   Liam Clarke, 15 years after Good Friday Agreement, and still no peace dividend for Northern Ireland, *Belfast Telegraph*, 9 April 2013. See also: Henry McDonald, Peace and poverty for Troubles survivors, *The Guardian*, 29 August 2014

19   Cfr. Colin Coulter (2014), Under Which Constitutional Arrangement Would You Still Prefer to be Unemployed? Neoliberalism, the Peace Process, and the Politics of Class in Northern Ireland, *Studies in Conflict & Terrorism*, 37:9, 763-776 and Goretti Horgan (2006) Devolution, Direct Rule and Neo-Liberal Reconstruction in Northern Ireland, *Critical Social Policy*, 26:3, 656-666

20   Suzanne Breen, 'I'll jail McGuinness any day soon', jokes Paisley, *Sunday Tribune*, 6 May 2007

21   Research shows Catholics gained more from NI peace process than Protestants, *Belfast Telegraph*, 31 March 2008

22   Tide of history with nationalists, *An Phoblacht-Republican News*, 27 October 1994; The fun isn't over, *An Phoblacht-Republican News*, 6 August 1998

23   Paul Nolan (2012), op.cit., 9

24   Claire Mitchell (2003), From Victims To Equals? Catholic Responses to Political Change in Northern Ireland, *Irish Political Studies*, 18:1, 51-71

25   Sarah Burns, Catholics face higher unemployment than Protestants in North, *Irish Times*, 31 January 2018

26   E.A Aunger (1983), Religion and Class: An Analysis of 1971 Census Data, in R.J Cormack and R.D. Osborne (eds) *Religion, Education and Employment: Aspects of Equal Opportunity in Northern Ireland*, Belfast: Appletree Press, 24-42

27 Richard Breen (2000), Class Inequality and Social Mobility in Northern Ireland 1973-1996, *American Sociological Review*, 65:3, 397

28 Meghan Cox Gurdon, N. Ireland's Minority Beats Back a Stereotype, *The Christian Science Monitor*, 27 March 1996

29 R.J Cormack and R.D. Osborne (1994), The Evolution of A Catholic Middle Class, in Adrian Guelke (ed), *New Perspectives on the Northern Ireland Conflict*, Aldershot: Avebury, 65 and 79

30 Richard Breen (2001), Social Mobility and Constitutional and Political Preferences in Northern Ireland, *British Journal of Sociology*, 52:4, 626

31 Paul Nolan (2013), op.cit., 93

32 Paul Bew (2007), *The Making and Remaking of the Good Friday Agreement*, op.cit., 71

33 Jim Cusack, Who's got the bling here – Catholics or Protestants?, *Belfast Telegraph*, 18 June 2008

34 Northern Ireland's place in the UK secure despite opposition to Brexit, says Arlene Foster, *Newsletter*, 24 June 2016

35 Theresa May: Word unionist *'very important to me'*, BBC website, 13 July 2016

36 The Protestant retreat, *The Economist*, 6 September 2001

37 Eamonn McCann, Northern Ireland's identity crisis, *The Guardian*, 18 June 2009

38 Paul Nolan (2012), op.cit., 105

39 Paul Nolan (2014), op.cit., 13

40 Reid warning over alienation, BBC website, 21 November 2001

41 Alastair Campbell (2012), *Diaries, Volume Three: Power and Responsibility*, London: Arrow Books, 66

42 Union is secure, says Robinson, *Belfast Telegraph*, 26 September 2014

43 See: P. Mitchell, B. O'Leary, G. Evans (2001), Flanking

extremists bite the moderates and emerge in their clothes, *Parliamentary Affairs*, 54:4, 725-742

44 Tony Catney, Sinn Féin's electoral growth, *Fourthwrite*, Issue 2, Summer 2000

45 P. Mitchell, G. Evans, B. O'Leary (2009), Extremist outbidding in ethnic party systems is not inevitable: tribune parties in Northern Ireland, *Political Studies*, 57:2, 403

46 Cathy Gormley-Heenan and Roger Macginty (2008) Ethnic Outbidding and Party Modernization: Understanding the Democratic Unionist Party's Electoral Success in the Post-Agreement Environment, *Ethnopolitics*, 7:1, 43-61

47 Henry McDonald, Unionists will hold vote veto, *The Observer*, 6 May 2007

48 Paul Bew (2007), *The Making and Remaking of the Good Friday Agreement*, op.cit., 140-143

49 Edward W. Said (1995), *Peace & Its Discontents*, op.cit., 2

50 Brendan Murtagh and Peter Shirlow (2012), Devolution and the politics of development in Northern Ireland, *Environment and Planning C: Government and Policy*, 30:1, 53

51 Goretti Horgan and Ann Marie Gray (2012), Devolution in Northern Ireland: A Lost Opportunity? *Critical Social Policy*, 32:3, 467-478

52 See in particular: Mike Burke, Stormont House Agreement, *The Pensive Quill* website, 1 January 2015

53 See: Peter Shirlow and Brendan Murtagh (2006), *Belfast: Segregation, Violence and the City*, London: Pluto Press

54 Paul Nolan (2012), op.cit., 147ff

55 Patsy McGarry, Barriers testify to political failure, *Irish Times*, 3 September 2011

56 William J.V. Neill (2006): Return to Titanic and lost in the Maze: The search for representation of 'post-conflict' Belfast, *Space and Polity*, 10:2, 119

57 Chris Gilligan (2007), The Irish question and the concept

of 'identity' in the 1980s, *Nations and Nationalism*, 13:4, 599-661 for a detailed study of this transformation

58   Ann Thomson (1991), Thomas Paine and the United Irishmen, *Études Irlandaises*, 16:1, 109-119; David Dickson (1993), Paine and Ireland, in David Dickson, Daire Keogh, and Kevin Whelan (eds), *The United Irishmen: Republicanism, Radicalism and Rebellion*, Dublin: Lilliput Press, 135-150. On the importance of Thomas Paine for republicans today, see Bernadette McAliskey, (2010) Opening Up Thomas Paine's *The Rights of Man*, in: Fiona Dukelow and Orla O'Donovan (eds), *Mobilising Classics: Reading Radical Writing in Ireland*, Manchester University Press, 8-20

59   Robbie McVeigh (2015), No-One Likes Us, We Don't Care: What is to be (un) done about Ulster Protestant Identity? in Thomas Paul Burgess and Gareth Mulvenna (eds) *The Contested Identities of Ulster Protestants*, Basingstoke: Palgrave Macmillan, 118-120

60   Gerry Adams, Governments fail to honour obligations on crucial issues, op.cit.

61   Kevin Bean and Mark Hayes (2009), Sinn Féin and the New Republicanism in Ireland: Electoral Progress, Political Stasis, and Ideological Failure, *Radical History Review*, Issue 104 (Spring 2009), 136

62   In terms of Sinn Féin see for example: Martin McGuinness, All identities and cultures need to be given respect, *Belfast Telegraph*, 18 January 2013; 'I respect Britishness. All I ask is respect in return': Martin McGuinness on cultural identity, *Belfast Telegraph*, 29 March 2013

63   Kevin Bean (2007), *The New Politics of Sinn Féin*, Liverpool University Press, Part II *passim*

64   A tongue-twister of a dispute, *The Economist*, 25 September 2008

65   Gilles Deleuze and Claire Parnet (1996), *Dialogues*, Paris: Flammarion, 11

66   Christopher Lasch (1979) *The Culture of Narcissism: American Life in an Age of Diminishing Expectations*, New York: W.W. Norton offered a diagnostic of the ills of US society that is highly relevant today in Northern Ireland

67   David Barsamian and Edward W. Said (2003), *Culture and Resistance: Conversations with Edward W. Said*, Cambridge, Mass.: South End Press, 190

68   Eamonn McCann, Rooting for England, *Sunday Journal*, 11 September 2005

69   Jason Walsh, How the 'peace process' provokes violence, *Spiked Online*, 11 December 2012

70   Kieran McEvoy and Peter Shirlow (2013), The Northern Ireland Peace Process and 'Terroristic' Narratives, *Terrorism and Political Violence*, 25:2, 164

71   Conversations with Jacqueline Rose (2010), London: Seagull Books, 93

72   B. P. Bunting, F. R. Ferry, S. D. Murphy, S. M. O'Neill and D. Bolton, D. (2013), Trauma Associated With Civil Conflict and Posttraumatic Stress Disorder: Evidence From the Northern Ireland Study of Health and Stress, *Journal of Trauma and Stress*, 26:1, 134-141

73   C. Downes, E. Harrison, D. Curran, M. Kavanagh (2013), The trauma still goes on...: the multigenerational legacy of Northern Ireland's conflict, Clinical Child Psychology and Psychiatry, 18:4, 583-603

74   Frank Furedi (2003), *Therapy Culture: Cultivating Vulnerability in an Uncertain Age*, London: Routledge, 4-7

75   Chris Gilligan (2006), Traumatised by peace? A critique of five assumptions in the theory and practice of conflict-related trauma policy in Northern Ireland, *Policy & Politics*, 34:2, 335 and 339-40

76   Bill Rolston (2007), Facing Reality: The media, the past and conflict transformation in Northern Ireland, *Crime Media Culture*, 3:3, 359

77 Jacques Derrida (1997), Cosmopolites de Tous les Pays, Encore un Effort!, Paris: Galilée, 38ff

78 Patricia Lundy and Bill Rolston (2016), Redress for past harms? Official apologies in Northern Ireland, *International Journal of Human Rights*, 20:1, 104-122

79 Paul de Man (1979), *Allegories of Reading: Figural Language in Rousseau, Nietzsche, Rilke and Proust*, New Haven: Yale University Press, 293 and 299

80 Mike Tomlinson (2012), From counter-terrorism to criminal justice: transformation or business as usual? *Howard Journal*, 51:5, 449

81 Brendan O'Neill, The moral hijacking of Bloody Sunday, *Spiked online*, 30 January 2012

82 Brendan O'Neill, Pat Finucane wasn't the only victim of collusion, *Spiked online*, 13 December 2012

83 Malachi O'Doherty, No shortcuts to an agreed past, *Belfast Telegraph*, 4 July 2014

84 John Brewer (2015), In Northern Ireland Not Every Murder is Treated the Same, http://theconversation.com/in-northern-ireland-not-every-murder-is-treated-the-same-42569

85 DPP has brought more cases against terrorists than the state, stats show, *The Newsletter*, 30 January 2017

86 Daniel Finn (2018), Irish Politics Since the Crash, 2008-2016, *boundary 2*, 45:1, 47

87 Zac Cope (2014), Labor in Transitional Societies: Conflict, Democracy and Neoliberalism, *Working USA: The Journal of Labor & Society*, 17:4, 455-489

Part Four. Real Peace or Simulation of Peace?

Philosophy, which once seemed obsolete, lives on because the moment to realize it was missed. The summary judgement that it had merely interpreted the world, that resignation on the face of reality had crippled it in itself, becomes a defeatism of reason after the attempt to change the world miscarried.
Theodor W. Adorno (1966), Negative Dialectics

Always historicize! This slogan (is) the one absolute and we may even say 'transhistorical' imperative of dialectical thought.
Fredric Jameson (1981), The Political Unconscious: Narrative as a Socially Symbolic Act

Retreat from politics

The year 2018 marked the twentieth anniversary of the Belfast Agreement. This study described Northern Ireland as a Potemkin Village of neo-liberal peace. Interestingly in preparation for hosting the June 2013 G8 summit in Northern Ireland, large photographs were put up in the windows of closed shops in a number of towns so as to give the appearance of thriving businesses for visitors driving past them[1]. 'Potemkin Village' is thus not just a figure of speech, it is an actual reality in Northern Ireland. The flagship in the neo-liberal re-branding of Northern Ireland is the £100 million Titanic Quarter in Belfast which opened on 31 March 2012. It is hardly surprising that there were criticisms of the fact that working-class communities living nearby have missed out on the dividend from development at Titanic Quarter[2]. The 'New Northern Ireland' ushered by the Belfast Agreement has fundamentally been a neo-liberal project.

Today in Northern Ireland the war is not only over but is becoming increasingly distant and of purely historcal and academic interest. The conflict has been converted into heritage and is being sold as a tourist attraction such as visiting murals or peace walls. There are now more racist than sectarian attacks[3]. In 2007 Ed Moloney pointed out that the peace process, its beginning dated by the first ceasefire of 1994, had lasted nearly three times longer than the First World War, twice as long as the Second World War, and virtually as long as American involvement in Vietnam, probably making the peace process in Northern Ireland one of the longest in human history. The main protagonists of the conflict are starting to pass away, as the deaths of Margaret Thatcher on 8 April 2013, Ian Paisley on 12 September 2014 and Martin McGuinness on 21 March 2017 illustrate. A child born in 1998 will be 20-years-old now, and there is at present an entire generation that has no living memory of the conflict. Mary Lou McDonald, who succeeded Gerry Adams as president of Sinn Féin on 10 February 2018, and Michelle O'Neill, who on 23 January 2017 replaced Martin McGuinness as Sinn Féin's leader in the Northern Ireland Assembly and was elected Vice-President of the party on 10 February 2018, both only joined the party after the 1998 Agreement. This represents a generational change and the arrival of a new generation of politicians with no background in the conflict. Not only is the war over, but the situation in Northern Ireland is politically moribund. To borrow Gramsci's expression, the horizon is no longer 'major politics' but what he defined as 'minor politics' – 'day-to-day politics, parliamentary politics, politics of lobbying and intrigue': 'High politics deals with questions related to the foundation of new states, and the struggle for the destruction, defense, and conservation of given organic socioeconomic structures. Minor politics is related to the partial and daily issues taken up within an already established structure for the struggle for primacy among different factions of the same political class[4].' Politics is no longer about questions such as '32 county democratic socialist republic versus United Kingdom' but how many days a year the Union Jack should float, whether or not there should be an Irish Language Act or so-called marriage equality. What one academic calls 'the capitalism of boredom' dominates the Northern Irish political scene[5]. The photograph of former political adversaries Martin McGuinness and Ian Paisley opening the first IKEA store in Northern Ireland on 13 December 2007 shows that what really matters now is no longer British or Irish sovereignty but the sovereignty of the consumer. The 'shared space' in the new Northern Ireland is mostly confined to retail space such as the Victoria Square Shopping Centre in Belfast which opened on 6 March 2008; ostensibly proving how 'peace' goes hand in hand with 'prosperity'. It is not surprising that since 1998 one can see that fewer and fewer people bother to take part in elections or political activites. If in 1998, 69.8 per cent of the electorate voted in elections in Northern Ireland, this fell to 54.2 per cent in 2016. On 23 June 2016, only 48.9 per cent of the electorate took part in the Brexit referendum in West Belfast, called by some the most politicised community in Western Europe. The retreat from politics is even sharper for younger people. An analysis by academics at Liverpool University's Institute of Irish Studies showed that about two-thirds of electors (65 per cent) between the ages of 18 and 24 did not bother to vote in June 2017's Westminster election[6]. The fact that so many do not bother to vote or be politically active shows how indifferent people have become to what passes as 'politics' in Northern Ireland. Asked if this developed because people are war weary, veteran republican Brendan Hughes replied that people are not just war weary: 'They are politics weary, the same old lies regurgitated week in week out. With the war politics had some substance. Now it has none[7].' There is no appetite for war and very little for politics. Parallel to the peace process there is also a process of depoliticisation reinforced by therapeutic culture and the victims industry.

The peace process in an age of austerity

Following the financial crisis of 2007-2008 the Great Recession began. In terms of overall impact, the International Monetary Fund concluded that it was the worst global recession since the 1930s (the Great Depression). The economic recession and the imposition of public spending cuts by Westminster have put strains on the devolved Assembly. According to research based on official figures Northern Ireland suffered the largest fall in household incomes and the biggest rise in poverty in the UK during the recession and austerity measures are hitting every facet of everyday life in the province after years of resisting UK-imposed budget reductions. Northern Ireland also has the slowest recovery from recession on record for the UK as a whole[8].

Michael McDowell, a former Tánaiste (deputy head of the Dublin government and the second-most senior officer in the Irish government), predicted in 2012 that the peace process will survive the economic downturn on both sides of the border. Politics in the North could become more divisive in the absence of economic progress, but he said he didn't believe there was a fundamental risk that it would slip back into conflict[9].

This raises the important question of the political effects of the economic crisis. There is no automatic connection between an economic and a political crisis. There is an economic crisis, but it has not yet reached the stage of an organic crisis – where the very legitimacy of the system itself is questioned. Instead, in the North the crisis has led to calls to lower corporation taxes. There was a substantial one-day strike on 30 November 2011 over public sector pensions and a one-day strike on 13 March 2015 to protest at budget cuts and looming job losses but they seem to have had little political effect. Such protests remain limited to what Gramsci would have called 'economic-corporate' interests and sectional demands of public sector workers.

Trade union density – that is the proportion of workers who are members of a union – is high in Northern Ireland standing at 34 per cent in 2017. Over half of all employees' pay is affected by a collective trade union agreement, the highest proportion anywhere in the UK. There are 243,000 trade union members in the region at the last count, the majority of whom are in the public sector. Over 70 per cent of these are members of 78 different Great Britain-based unions[10]. In 2016 the number of workers going on strike in the United Kingdom was the lowest since records began in 1893. Despite the high trade union density, Northern Ireland had the lowest strike rate of 2016, with 4 working days lost per 1000 employees, proving Mick Hume's remark that this is the age of the general shrug, not the general strike. Northern Ireland illustrates Adorno's point in *Minima Moralia*: 'Sociologists, however, ponder the grimly comic riddle: where is the proletariat?[11]'

The very concept of politically 'left-wing' or 'right-wing' remains very marginal in Northern Ireland. In a major opinion survey in 2014, only 25 per cent of respondents were able to describe their political views as either 'left-wing' or 'right-wing'. And 34 per cent said they didn't know how to categorise their views in these terms or were able to characterise the policies of the different political parties in these terms[12]. That said there have been indications of a slight shift to the left. Since Jeremy Corbyn was elected party leader on 12 September 2015 membership of the Labour Party in Northern Ireland jumped tenfold from 300 to 3000 for example. But the most visible sign of political opposition to austerity measures has been the growth of People Before Profit, an anti-capitalist party aligned to the International Socialist Tendency of Tony Cliff. In the 2007 Assembly elections, prior to the Great Recession, the party had received a mere 774 votes (0.1 per cent). But its candidate in the Belfast West constituency during the 5 May 2016 Northern Ireland Assembly Election went on spectaculary to top the poll there with 8299 votes (22.9 per cent), almost 4000 first-preference votes clear of his nearest challenger from Sinn Féin which is remarkable. During that election, People Before Profit also secured a seat in the Derry constituency of Foyle. Overall the party in 2016 received 13,761 votes (2 per cent of the poll) compared to 5438 votes (0.8 per cent) and no elected candidates in 2011. In the 2017 Northern Ireland Assembly Elections, the party retained its West Belfast seat but with a much-reduced vote (12.2 per cent), while losing its other one in Derry. Overall it received 14,100 votes (1.8 per cent). Since 2014 it also has one local councillor elected in Belfast. Claiming to be neither nationalist nor unionist but socialist, it is not clear at this stage whether People Before Profit will grow further or have a lasting political impact.

The limited electoral success of People Before Profit shows that the Great Recession has not enabled the emergence of a new political force in Northern Ireland capable of seriously challenging austerity – like Podemos in Spain or Syriza in Greece. The consociational framework and 'ethnic outbidding' system of Northern Irish politics are clear obstacles to that[13]. However, in March 2015, Syriza's Euclid Tsakalotos had addressed a Sinn Féin conference with this rousing message: 'Syriza, Sinn Féin, Podemos and others are part of a great realignment in European politics that has become apparent over the last couple of years.' For Sinn Féin member of the European Parliament Martina Anderson, the affinity between the parties was clear: 'Republicanism is on the rise. In Athens it's called Syriza, in Spain it's called Podemos, in Ireland it's called Sinn Féin[14].'

However, while Sinn Féin praises Alexis Tsiparas or Yanis Varoufakis, the party is advocating a lower corporation tax in Northern Ireland as one of the main drivers to solve the region's economic problems; and while it backs austerity measures in the north of Ireland it rejects them in the South. Although it is in charge of implementing neo-liberal austerity measures in Northern Ireland, the party has been able to grow electorally in the Republic of Ireland by opposing austerity measures there. In 1997, Sinn Féin had a single TD (member of the Irish Parliament) elected to the Dáil, the party's first in 40 years and had received a total of 45,614 votes (2.5 per cent). Close to 20 years later, during the 26 February 2016 general elections in the Republic of Ireland, 23 Sinn Féin TDs were elected and the party secured 295,319 votes (13.8 per cent) on an anti-austerity platform. The context had changed since 1997 and the 'Celtic Tiger', when just 5 days after the recession of the Irish economy was officially declared, on 30 September 2008 the Dublin government decided to issue a blanket guarantee for the €440 billion worth of debt of Irish banks and later on 29 November 2010 the Dublin government entered the bailout programme.

In November 2017, a Sinn Féin Ard Fheis approved a proposal that it will be ready to be a junior – or senior – partner to Fianna Fáil or Fine Gael in any potential coalition government in the Dáil. A motion put before the June 2018 Sinn Féin Ard Fheis said the party's only objective after the next election should be the formation of a left-wing government. However it was amended by the Ard Comhairle, the party's executive council, to relegate the importance of a left-wing government to an attempted rather than binding objective. The fact that the party is now prepared to accept becoming a junior partner in a future right-wing coaltion indicates that it is toning down its ambitions and questions the extent to which it will oppose austerity measures. In response to the party softening its stance on a possible coalition with Fianna Fáil or Fine Gael, Sinn Féin was ditched as a potential government partner by Solidarity–People Before Profit; an electoral alliance of the Irish section of the Committee for a Workers' International and People Before Profit which secured 3.9 per cent of the vote and had six TDs elected during the 2016 general elections. This indicates that Sinn Féin's left credentials are starting to be seriously questioned down south. But getting into coalition government with Fianna Fáil or Fine Gael wouldn't be a step too far for a party which has already been a junior partner to the Democratic Unionist Party and who will go down in history as having put Ian Paisley in power. The Northern Ireland Assembly collapsed on 9 January 2017. It is not in Sinn Féin's interest to have an Assembly running again and having to impose austerity measures while campaigning down south against such measures. If Sinn Féin enters the Dublin government in the near future, based on its performance in Northern Ireland, the overall probability is that it is going to be transformed by the status quo rather than the party transforming it. While the party is unlikely to succeed in achieving a united Ireland, it will probably claim that being in government in both parts of Ireland should bring reunification closer. In the title of an article quoted earlier, Kevin Bean and Mark Hayes described the endgame for Sinn Féin in Northern Ireland as one of 'electoral progress, political stasis, and ideological failure' and the same is likely to apply to their fortunes in the Republic of Ireland.

The Great Recession has not undermined the peace process, although it has made it much more difficult to transform Northern Ireland into an economic model of neo-liberal peace. While austerity measures have increased discontent towards the status quo to some extent, the very legitimacy of the economic, social and political system itself has not been challenged. But as Fredric Jameson and Slavoj Žižek have said, today it is easier to imagine the end of the world than the end of capitalism[15]. Popular movements which have risen elsewhere in the western world as a response to the crisis – Occupy, Indignados, Podemos, Syriza and others – have had limited impact within Northern Ireland. The nature of the crisis has essentially been economic, not political. As Michel Houellebecq stated in his 2010 novel *La Carte et le Territoire* (*The Map and the Territory*):

> More generally, you were living in an ideologically strange period, when everyone in Western Europe seemed persuaded that capitalism was doomed, and even doomed in the short term, that it was living through its very last years, without, however, the far-left parties managing to attract anyone beyond their usual clientele of spiteful masochists. A veil of

ashes seemed to have spread over people's minds[16].

Brexit

The peace process and the 1998 Agreement achieved the 'reconstitution of bourgeois order' in the North 'not in the context of the British Empire...but in the context of the European Union[17]'. In 1998 the United Kingdom and Ireland were, in the words of the Belfast Agreement, 'partners in the European Union'. The EU was credited with providing the framework that made the peace process and the political institutions possible. But on 23 June 2016 the people of the United Kingdom voted in a referendum 51.9 per cent to leave the European Union against 48.1 per cent to remain in the EU. In Northern Ireland 55.8 per cent of voters opted to remain in the European Union and 44.2 per cent to leave it. Only 62.69 per cent of registered voters took part in the referendum, against a UK average of 72.2 per cent, but this was the highest turn out since 1998: for example just a month prior to that on 5 May 2016 only 54.9 per cent of the electorate took part in the Northern Ireland Assembly elections. The United Kingdom will leave the EU's customs union and single market on 29 March 2019, and the British government is promising that there will be no new customs checks or physical infrastructure at the Irish border, or any between Northern Ireland and Britain. Stretching 499 kilometers (310 miles), the Irish border is the only land border between the United Kingdom and the European Union, it has more crossings than along the entire border between the European Union and the countries to its east, which has 137 compared to 208 in Ireland. For example, if you drive the 11 kilometers (seven miles) between Clones and Belturbet in county Monaghan, you will cross the border with county Fermanagh four times in about 9 minutes[18].

If the UK leaves the single market and diverges from EU regulatory standards, goods crossing the Irish border would need to be checked. But no one, including the Northern Ireland committee of Britain's Parliament, has yet identified technology that could enforce customs controls without any infrastructure. Before the 2016 referendum, the border between the two parts of Ireland had been made 'invisible' by the abolition of customs controls in 1993 and of security checks after the 1998 Agreement, with 30,000 border crossings every day, about half of those relating to business and education. In 2017 cross-border trade was worth more than €3 billion a year. Brexit changes this with the threat of a 'hard' border with customs checks and physical infrastructure.

Take the example of a globally known Irish brand, Guinness beer, to concretely illustrate the impact a hard border would have. The Guinness brewed in Dublin is bottled and canned in Belfast before being sent back to Dublin for distribution. That means what's in almost every bottle and can of the stout crosses the border twice before reaching beer drinkers. A so-called 'hard border' could cause delays of between 30 minutes and an hour, costing an extra €100 (£85) for each lorry-load of Guinness. Each year the company makes 13,000 beer-related border crossings in Ireland and Guinness contingency plans estimate the delays could amount to €1.3m in additional costs a year. The company would either be forced to absorb that cost or pass it on to the consumer by raising the cost of a pint. If that happened, the price of Guinness might have to rise[19].

Theresa May triggered Article 50 on 29 March 2017, starting negotiations on the UK's exit from the EU. Brexit talks on Ireland aren't just about the border, there are 142 areas of North-South co-operation that also cover things ranging from trade and tourism to eel migration. Her government has not found a solution on how to maintain a 'soft' border[20]. Brexit Secretary David Davis admitted in April 2018 that a solution for the Irish border problem may not be found until after the UK has left the European Union. Given there is a transition period agreed with the UK remaining in the customs union until January 2021, a final solution for the Northern Ireland border does not need to be fully in place until that period ends.

About 60 per cent of Northern Ireland's exports are to the EU, and of that more than half go to the Republic of Ireland, making it likely to suffer the greatest negative economic impact from Brexit, given its closer economic relationship with the EU and the Republic of Ireland, compared with other parts of the UK. The EU had a determining impact on Northern Ireland's environmental and social protection legislation and Brexit brings a threat of the North accelerating in a race to the bottom in terms of the environment and employment, cutting costs in order to get economic advantage[21].

Much media comment has centred on the assertion that Brexit threatens the 1998 Agreement and peace process in Northern Ireland. Similar views are also expressed by elements of the political classes in Dublin, Brussels and London. But British departure from the European Union will have no effect on the letter of the 1998 Agreement. This has been established conclusively by the highest courts in Northern Ireland and Britain. The climate and conditions which gave rise to the so-called 'Troubles' no longer exist. There is currently very little appetite for a resumption of an armed campaign and the triggering of Article 50 has not changed this. As the Political Editor of the *Belfast Telegraph* puts it:

There are many legitimate concerns around Brexit and its effects on both sides of the border. But claiming it's a ticking time bomb for the peace process is quite simply scaremongering. The customs checkpoints which existed along the border for almost half a century after partition played no part in violence erupting here in 1969. That IRA campaign was firmly rooted in the denial of civil rights – jobs, housing and political equality. A return to the border as we knew it from the 1970s onwards – with British soldiers in watchtowers on the hillsides above checkpoints – is not on the cards. Of course, the introduction of any infrastructure will serve as a reminder – and perhaps an uncomfortable one for some – that partition and the border still do exist. But the youth of Ballymurphy or the Bogside will not go out to kill or be killed because of customs controls. And who exactly are expected to wage any new armed campaign anyway? The Provisionals' war is over. Dissident republicans are having some success in recruiting young people in working-class nationalist areas, but I guarantee that none of those joining up are citing Brexit and the possibility of customs posts as their reasons[22].

Former IRA volunteers agree with this analysis and believe the threat of a return to conflict is essentially a scare tactic to force the issue of the border to the centre of the Brexit negotiations[23].

The Brexit debate has resurrected the Irish border issue close to 100 years after it was set up. It provides an injection of reality: the border hasn't gone away and will be physically manifested again. It shows the politcal reality of partition. Brexit entrenches partition as the border will be not just that between the United Kingdom and the Republic of Ireland but also one between the UK and the European Union. Brexit also reminds us of the existence of English nationalism which played a key role in the campaign to leave the EU. With the DUP confidence-and-supply support for a Conservative minority government, unionism is now at the heart of government. In 2016 Bernadette McAliskey stated: 'I voted Remain notwithstanding all the things that I know about the European Union. You have to make the decision in this context, in this time: does it bring us forward or back?' She didn't 'really see how strengthening the Little Englander mentality with the whole imperialist history behind it and a racist agenda' would strengthen the left position[24]. As Étienne Balibar has stated, Brexit is the anti-Grexit[25].

Six counties border poll or all-Ireland referendum?

Sylvia Hermon, Northern Ireland's only anti-Brexit unionist MP, told the BBC in May 2018 that she now believes she will see a border poll there in her lifetime because of the decision to leave the European Union: 'I am worried about the consequences of Brexit. In my lifetime I never thought that I would see a border poll and I am now convinced that I probably will see a border poll[26].' Brexit also could trigger a new independence referendum in Scotland where 62 per cent voted to remain part of the European Union. On 27 June 2017, Nicola Sturgeon declared however that her government would 'reset' the referendum plan to delay it until after the Brexit process has finished. Brexit thus increases the crisis of the British state.

The majority of voters in Northern Ireland voted to remain in the EU, fuelling Sinn Féin to say a united Ireland would save them from Brexit and prompting the party to call for a border poll. Sinn Féin's call for a border poll had already been encouraged by the Scottish independence referendum on 18 September 2014 and more recently by the Catalan one on 1 October 2017. Sinn Féin claims there is now a democratic imperative for a border poll and a unity referendum within 5 years is a central objective of the party in 2018[27].

The question of whether Ireland is united or not is not really in the hands of Irish people: the British state still holds the cards in terms of whether it is or not. Under the current legislation (Schedule 1 of the 1998 Northern Ireland Act), the authority to call a border poll on whether Northern Ireland should cease to be part of the United Kingdom rests with the Northern Ireland Secretary of State, who shall exercise the power 'if at any time it appears likely to him that a majority of those voting would express a wish that Northern Ireland should cease to be part of the United Kingdom and form part of a United Ireland'. The poll would be restricted to people inside the British created border of Northern Ireland and it is the British state who ultimately decides whether any such border poll is held. Following the Brexit vote, the demand for a border poll was immediately rejected not only by British Prime Minister David Cameron and Northern Ireland Secretary of State Theresa Villiers, but also by Taoiseach (Prime Minister of the Irish government) Enda Kenny and his Foreign Affairs minister Charlie Flanagan. Moreover, different Irish prime ministers have stated that a simple majority in a border poll would not be enough to secure a united Ireland, raising the question as to what would count as a 'majority' and who would decide this[28].

But a number of indicators would encourage Sinn Féin to believe 'that a majority of those voting would express a wish that Northern Ireland should cease to be part of the United Kingdom and form part of a United Ireland' and that the Protestant majority in Northern Ireland will come to an end in 2021 – on the one hundredth anniversary of partition. With that in mind, in April 2018 DUP First Minister Arlene Foster told a BBC programme that she would 'probably leave' the country if a border poll resulted in a united Ireland. Census figures from 2011 showed a narrowing gap between the two religions, putting the Protestant population at 48 per cent, just 3 per cent ahead of the Catholic one (45 per cent). Figures from 2016 show that among those of working age, 44 per cent are now Catholic and 40 per cent Protestant. The difference is even more marked among school children, with 51 per cent Catholic and 37 per cent Protestant. Only among the over-60s is there a clear majority of Protestants, with 57 per cent compared to 35 per cent of Catholics. 'It would be a considerable irony…if it turns out that a state that was set up to provide security for the Protestant of Ulster by providing them with a permanent in-built majority should, 100 years on from its creation, end up with a Catholic population larger than the Protestant one[29].'

More significantly, unionists in 2017 lost their majority in the local Assembly for the first time since the creation of Northern

Ireland a century ago. Unionism, which had enjoyed almost a century of almost unchallenged dominance at Stormont, was reduced after the dramatic 2 March 2017 elections to a combined total of 38 seats in the new 90-seat Assembly as against a combined total of 39 held by Sinn Féin and the SDLP, while others have 11 seats. The two main unionist parties, the DUP and UUP, jointly now have 38 seats in a 90-seat Assembly, while Sinn Féin and the SDLP have 39. What was once a 10-seat gap between Sinn Féin and the DUP is now only a single seat, with only 1168 votes separating the DUP from Sinn Féin in being the largest party. Dropping below 30 seats, the DUP also lost the petition of concern on legislation, affecting a power of veto. It was the end of the unionist majority in a parliamment and a building which had been for so long the symbol of unionist domination of Northern Ireland. 'The resulting loss of a Unionist majority at Stormont for the first time has shocked unionism to its core. The political and, especially, the psychological implications of this as the centenary of Partition approaches in 2021 should not be underestimated[30].'

While the idea of unionist majority coming to an end on the hundredth anniversary of partition is interesting, this does not mean that a united Ireland (never mind the 32-county democratic socialist republic) is any closer. There is no reason to believe that the Remain vote would translate into support for a united Ireland. There is little evidence that Brexit has fuelled any great eruption of desire for the reunification of Ireland, even if Irish passport application numbers in Northern Ireland and the UK have risen substantially. Indeed, recent surveys show that support for Irish unity has never been lower. Since 1998 it has consistently diminished. The recent Northern Ireland Life and Times survey claimed 44 per cent of Catholic respondents wanted to remain in the United Kingdom, with just 35 per cent admitting to wanting a united Ireland. In contrast, just 19 per cent of Catholics questioned by the same survey team in 1998 favoured the UK connection, while 49 per cent claimed they wanted a united Ireland[31]. It is clear that not all Sinn Féin supporters, let alone all Catholics, would vote for unification. A poll in 2015 found that 30 per cent of Northern Irish would be in favour – and when respondents were told that it would mean higher taxes (a near certainty, as the Dublin government could not afford the £10 billion of subsidies that Britain shovels to Northern Ireland each year), the figure dropped to 11 per cent. Support for it in the Republic of Ireland dropped from 66 per cent to 31 per cent when the financial implications were pointed out[32]. Opinion polls have found no evidence that Brexit has yet caused a radical shift in public opinion which would make a referendum on a united Ireland remotely winnable. In May 2018 an Ipsos MORI poll commissioned by academics at Queen's University Belfast for a major piece of research funded by the Economic and Social Research Council, entitled *Northern Ireland and the UK's Exit from the EU: What do people think?*, found that not even half of Catholics would vote for a united Ireland, with just 42.6 per cent of Catholics favouring that option – although a large percentage, 26 per cent, were undecided.

It is important to emphasize that the demographic shift in favour of Catholics has not translated into any significant advance in the nationalist vote since the Belfast Agreement. Between the June 1998 Assembly election and the March 2017 Assembly election, 76,153 voters were added to the electorate. And yet over this 19-year period the combined nationalist vote (that is, the SDLP and SF vote taken together) has only risen by 0.1 of a percentage point: from 39.7 per cent in the June 1998 Assembly election to 39.8 per cent in the March 2017 Assembly election. The overall nationalist vote remains stuck at this level and rather than breaking through the 50 per cent barrier it finds it hard to break the 40 per cent ceiling[33].

Finally if the combined DUP-UUP vote in the 2 March 2017 elections was just 8524 votes ahead of the combined Sinn Féin-

SDLP vote, 2 months later in the Westminster General Election on 8 June 2017 the combined unionist vote was 41,262 votes ahead of the combined nationalist vote. The difference between the combined nationalist and unionist vote is even greater if the 64,553 votes for the 'soft' unionist Alliance Party are included. The idea of the loss of the unionist political majority is exaggerated and should be greatly nuanced.

It is interesting that on 14 May 2018 Theresa May stated in Parliament that she was 'not confident' unionists would win an Irish border poll. The current British administration stated that month that 'the circumstances requiring a border poll are not satisfied' and concentrates on trying to re-establish a devolved administration in Stormont which has been suspended since 9 January 2017 following the Renewable Heating Initiative scandal[34]. Bernadette McAliskey has claimed that a border poll isn't on the cards and that Sinn Féin knows it's a non-starter. She said the party made its call for a referendum on Irish unity 'in the comfort that it won't happen. It's a deliberate distraction away from the realities we are facing today. The raising of the profile of the border poll is just part of the game-playing. There isn't going to be one.' The party's leaders had called for a poll in the belief that there wouldn't be a referendum. She added: 'In the outside chance that there was one, they're assured that they would be safe enough because it wouldn't be carried this time. It would improve the position and would set them up for the next time. But Sinn Féin has no intention of moving forward to a united Ireland that it doesn't control[35].'

On 8 March 1973, the last time a border poll was organised in Northern Ireland, it was opposed and boycotted by all anti-unionist groups, including the SDLP. The boycott was remarkably effective: 41 per cent of the electorate abstained. Republicans argue that national self-determination cannot be achieved by a border poll limited to the six counties. This confuses 'the right of the people of Ireland' with the 'right of the people of

Northern Ireland' to the democratic entitlement to decide their own constitutional future. At worst it is just a form of sectarian headcount. Since 2010, the 1916 Societies, a republican pressure group, has argued that a border poll would be partitionist in nature and says any vote on the border should take place on an all-Ireland basis. The 1916 Societies 'One Ireland-One Vote - All Ireland Referendum Now!' calls for an All-Ireland Border poll rather than just a poll in Northern Ireland. Des Dalton, President of Republican Sinn Féin, also criticises Sinn Féin's call for a border poll: 'The call for a "Border Poll" is more of the smoke and mirrors designed to give their supporters the illusion of actually doing something to end partition while masking the reality that they have been absorbed wholesale into the machinery of British rule.' However he was also critical of the 'One Ireland-One Vote' campaign: 'The right to exercise national self-determination should not be confused with holding a referendum to determine if such a right exists in the first place. You cannot put to a ballot something that is fundamental to our very definition as a nation[36].' But in the context of Scotland he adds: 'While as Irish Republicans we believe that the right to nationhood is inalienable and does not stand or fall on the basis of a referendum, we respected the right of the people of Scotland to use this mechanism to support for independence[37].' This explains Republican Sinn Féin's support for the independence referendum in Catalonia last year[38].

The 2014 referendum in Scotland reinforced the crisis of the British state, and along with the 2017 independence referendum in Catalonia brought back fundamental questions such as what is sovereignty or self-determination and the nature of the nation. At the time of writing it remains uncertain if and when an independence referendum will take place in Scotland; however, where it differs from Ireland is that there is no dispute on the legitimate unit of self-determination – a six counties border poll or an all-Ireland referendum. Also the decision to call a second

Scottish independence referendum does not depend on a British Secretary of State like in Northern Ireland. If Scotland becomes independent it is likely to have a detrimental effect on unionism. The issue of a six counties border poll, and how it differs from an all-Ireland referendum and how this relates to self-determination and the concept of nation, has brought to light the different and contradictory understandings that different republican organisations have of all those fundamental political concepts.

The 'respectable minority': 'dissidents' and dissenters

The 'propaganda of peace' insists that those who support 'peace' consequently also support the 'process', and that those who are critical of the 'process' are thus hostile to 'peace' and support going back to armed conflict. This is where so-called 'dissident' republicanism comes in. 'Dissident Republicans' is a term used by the media to refer in general to republicans who are critical of the 'peace process' and opposed to the Belfast Agreement, and those who support the use of force in particular.[39]

The state has even introduced the concept of 'VDR' – 'violent dissident republicans'. But the expression is problematic[40]. The term 'dissident' comes from the Latin 'dis-sedere', which means 'to break away from'. But one cannot say that republicans opposed to the Belfast Agreement broke away from republicanism. On the contrary, as Eamonn McCann points out, they 'do not dissent from the Republican tradition. What they dissent from is departure from the tradition[41]'. They define their ideology from 'traditional republican' to 'revolutionary republicanism' but not 'dissident'.

Following Sinn Féin's departure from the high ground of the republic to the practical acceptance of partititionist institutions, a number of organisations vowed to continue the armed struggle. However, their campaign took a fatal blow just 4 months after the 1998 Agreement when on 15 August 1998 a RIRA car bomb exploded in Omagh killing 29 people (including a woman

147

pregnant with twins and Spanish school children visiting the town) and injured some 220 others. The organisation did not intend to kill civilians, and many questions about the Omagh bomb remain unanswered, including the role of intelligence agencies in the atrocity[42]. The political effects of the Omagh bomb, one of the worst incidents of the conflict, was to strengthen the peace process rather than derail it. Public outrage was so high that it made pursuing armed struggle impossible. It meant that if you were critical of the peace process and the Belfast Agreement your practical alternative was the Omagh bomb.

One has to mention that this attempt to resume armed struggle happens in the context of the death of actually existing armed national liberation movements as a historical force, the last remnants of that tendency in Western Europe died when ETA in the Basque country declared 'a definite cessation of its armed activity' on 20 October 2011 and announced its dissolution on 3 May 2018 and the Corsican FLNC announced on 25 June 2014 'an immediate and unequivocal process of demilitarisation and gradual exit from clandestinity'. It is interesting to note that on 23 January 2018, Óglaigh na hÉireann – an armed group which had emerged in July 2008 – declared 'the environment is not right for armed conflict' at this present time and suspended its military operations against the British state[43].

While it has pockets of support (particularly in Ardoyne, Derry and the north west and north Armagh area) there is no significant level of support for physical force republicanism. Research suggested that in 2010 some 14 per cent of the nationalist population in Northern Ireland had some sympathy for it[44]. They represent what James Connolly called the 'respectable minority[45]'. Not only is the political climate hostile to a resumption of armed struggle, but the minority oppositional republican currents who reject the Belfast Agreement are very fragmented: there are currently at least five different political groups and four separate armed organisations, not to mention independent republicans not aligned to any of these groups. While some of them have been set up on real political principles, others have only come about because of personal network and localistic ties. Their attitude to socialism ranges from hostility to explicit support. These four separate armed organisations carried out a total of 39 operations (referred to by the British state as 'national security incidents') in 2010, 26 in 2011, 24 in 2012, 25 in 2013, 22 in 2014, 16 in 2015, 14 in 2016 and 5 in 2017. Successful operations are the exception not the rule. Since 1998 they have killed just two British soldiers, two police officers and two prison guards. Reliable sources estimate three-quarters to four-fifths of 'dissident' attacks are being thwarted[46]. None of the several groups committed to armed struggle are capable of waging a sustained campaign. As Ciarán Mac Lochlainn, the former commander of RIRA prisoners in HMP Maghaberry, stated: 'What presently exists is something between an illusion of war and an aspiration to wage war, but there is no war[47].'

Those limited armed actions set limits upon the British state's ability to 'normalise' Northern Ireland. This indicates that current armed actions have very much a symbolic value rather than a purely strategic one. It is interesting that in his 2007 Oxford history of Ireland, Professor Paul Bew noted how from a military point of view, Robert Emmett's 1803 insurrection was insignificant, but the 1803 insurrection was above all a blow against the British government's policy of 'normalisation' and 'amnesia' following the Act of Union[48]. This bears some striking resemblance to today's actions. However, the main victims of what the state refers to as 'violent dissident republicans' have been individuals accused of being criminals. From 2007 alleged criminals comprised more than 77 per cent of the 175 people shot dead or wounded by armed 'dissident' republicans. By contrast, police officers accounted for just over 15 per cent of shooting casualties from 2007 to 2015, while over the same period British soldiers who were shot made up just over 0.5 per cent of the overall casualty list[49].

It has to be emphasised that so-called 'punishment shootings' against alleged criminals, drug dealers, rapists etc are highly controversial among republican activists, many of whom are opposed to it[50]. Republican prisoners have criticised this vigilantism as the product of a moral panic rather than principled anti-imperialism[51]. Not only can the politics of so-called 'dissident' republican organisations be criticised for their vigilantist and commemorative nature but their activities are limited to what Dr Paddy Hoey calls 'the four Ps': 'critique of the peace process, policing, parades and prisoners[52]'. This shows a restricted understanding of the nature and scope of Irish republicanism. But it brings back the question of what is fundamental to republicanism: is it simply the 'pike in the thatch' tradition or is it the most advanced thinking tradition?

Dr Hoey distinguishes what the media calls Irish republican 'dissidents' from what he terms 'dissenters[53]'. While for 'dissidents' an armed campaign is fundamental, for dissenters, it is the 'process' that republicans are fundamentally opposed to, not the 'peace'. 'Neither Stormont nor Omagh' can describe their position. Their fundamental objection against the peace process is not that it has taken the gun out of Irish politics but that it has taken radical politics out of Irish republicanism. This study joins those republicans who are critical of the peace process, but who also refuse a return to armed struggle considered futile in present circumstances. The imperative is to forge the 'weapons of criticism' and not the 'criticism of weapons'. Republicans opposed to the 1998 Agreement are not against 'peace', but against 'peace at any price'; and in their view the process and Agreement are precisely peace at the wrong price. This study supports that conclusion.

Negative peace or peace with justice?

Some will say that whatever the defaults of the peace process, the main 'dividend' is that it is fortunate that it is only on rare occasions that people are killed for political reasons in Northern Ireland today. In its May 2018 annual statistic report, the PSNI stated that there had been a total of two 'security-related' deaths for the year 2017-2018. In all, by April 2018, a total of 158 people died in what the PSNI refer to as security-related killings in the 20 years since the Belfast Agreement was signed in April 1998, mostly during the first 5 years. But a study also calculated that a total of 2,400 potential lives have been saved since the Belfast Agreement by extrapolating the number of deaths recorded between 1969 and 1998 and then estimating how many people would have died since 1998 if the conflict had continued[54]. However, one should not confuse 'peace' with the abscence of open conflict. The welcome fact that political killings are few and uncommon is explained by the absence of open conflict, and not by the existence of a lasting peace and can be explained independently of the 'process'. What exists could be best called a 'negative peace', in the sense that there is no longer an open conflict in Northern Ireland but no reconciliation between historical enemies[55]. It is more accurate to speak of 'conflict cessation' than 'conflict resolution'. The 'process' is fundamentally about 'conflict management'. As Bernadette McAliskey pointed out, the aim of the process 'is to eradicate republicanism, not violence[56]'.

Here are the main conclusions to which this study has arrived. First, there are tensions between the dynamic of the peace process and the concept of truth. To 'truth' is preferred something called 'constructive ambiguity'. As Eamonn McCann stated in 2015: 'Underlying the dysfunctionality of the Stormont institutions is the fact that the peace process cannot handle the truth[57].' The process is not founded on truth and tolerates lies if they help further it. Second, the process is not based on the recognition of the right of self-determination of the people of Ireland as a whole, and therefore is unable to promote a peace that is grounded in justice. Indeed, some have recently argued that the people of Northern Ireland must choose between peace and justice. 'In places torn by war, there is all too often a choice to be made between justice and peace. We may want both; we may cry out for both. But the bleak truth is, we cannot have both[58].' The process is not founded on justice and a reflection on what Edward W. Said called 'a just peace[59]' is at best insufficient and at worst abscent. Third, the peace process goes hand in hand with a social and economic process of neo-liberal reconstruction that failed to bring 'dividends' to the people who were most affected by the conflict. An article published in The Guardian on the twentieth anniversary of the 1994 ceasefire reminded us that: 'People living in areas where republican and Loyalist violence was at its most intense in Northern Ireland are the socio-economic losers of the peace process.' If one of the benefits of the peace process is that everyone is supposed to be 'equal', the fact is that 'some are more equal than others[60]'. The process is not based on social and economic equality. More generally 2 decades on from the Belfast Agreement, the Northern Ireland economy 'continues to be highly dysfunctional'. 'The peace dividend hasn't quite manifested itself as an economic one,' concluded the Irish Times in 2017[61]. Fourth, the process defines the central problem as being that of competing ethno-national identities rather than one of unfinished decolonisation. This keeps an equal stance between unequal causes. The process fails to deal with the colonial legacy. A study published in 1998 noted that: 'The present process looks very little like a decolonisation process…(Northern Ireland) will continue to be a colonial rather than a post-colonial social formation[62].' Flowing from those four points is the implication that the process is criticised in the name of peace based on truth, justice, equality and universal emancipation. For reconciliation to be possible, it needs to go hand in hand with those values and never at their expense. Justice lies in the gap between conciliation and reconciliation.

In a Palestinian context, for Edward W. Said to criticise the process in the name of justice 'meant in effect taking a position against "hope" and "peace"'. 'To say such things at the time put one in a small minority, but I felt for intellectual and moral reasons it had to be done[63].' The same goes for the Irish process and 1998 Agreement. Bernadette McAliskey noted in a speech on 12 March 1994 in the early days of the process that to state, 'I think we're going the wrong way,' when 'the peace process is now a very popular and responsible one' means, 'I find myself as a minority of the minority of the minority ad infinitum.' But it was important to take this stance for moral and political reasons:

> Up until this point whatever disagreements one had with the Republican Movement, one could not question their fundamental integrity. But when people start throwing that into the balance and say, 'Look, in order to play politics you have to read between the lines. Read my lips and guess the noise I am making,' I have to say, 'I have to tell you boys, you're going down a wee tunnel. It won't bring you peace. It won't bring you equality and, when you come outside at the other end of it, you won't even have the personal and political integrity you had going into it[64].

A good term to characterise a peace to which truth, justice and equality are subordinated is 'pacification'. It is thus more accurate to speak of a 'pacification process' in Northern Ireland than a 'peace process'[65]. It is more a case of a 'simulation of peace[66]' than a real one.

Strategic failure or new phase of the struggle?

From the perspective of the British state, the process was a major success as it compelled republicans to accept what were its terms for the resolution of the conflict since 1973. For Bernadette McAliskey, from a republican point of view, the process could only be 'ideologically wrong and tactically stupid' as its fundamental aim was 'the de-militarisation, the de-radicalisation, the de-mobilisation of the resistance movement in the North[67]'. The political danger represented by Irish republicanism was neutralised. When on 26 June 2012 former IRA chief of staff Martin McGuinness shook the hand of the British Queen, he was not 'standing in front of the British head of state on equal terms, as head of another state that had gained its independence from Britain. He is there as deputy head of a state over which the British hold unalloyed sovereignty and which he ostensibly spent much of his adult life trying to destroy[68]'. The same thing can be said of Gerry Adams when he met Prince Charles on 19 May 2015. This sums up where the peace process led republicans to.

Republicans have taken the habit to describe their strategic failure as some 'new phase of the struggle'. This sounds like General Oliver P. Smith of the United States Marine Corps who during the Korean War said: 'We're not retreating, Hell! We're just attacking in a different direction.' But for republican veteran Tommy Gorman, this 'new phase of the struggle' only indicates the failure of the republican leadership:

In the early days our struggle was depicted as an odyssey of sorts and that, along the way we would come to and pass various milestones and road signs keeping us on track and giving us a clear vision of progress made towards the socialist republic.

- An end to partition
- No return to Stormont Rule
- The disbandment of the RUC
- A declaration of intent by the British Government to withdraw from Ireland

Through their efforts Sinn Féin have managed, in collaboration with other right-wing partners, to negotiate:

- The copper-fastening of partition
- A resurrected Stormont
- A renamed RUC
- A declaration of their intent to stay by the British Government.

In their eagerness to once again shore up a coalition of the unwilling to administer bad British rule in Ireland Sinn Féin has allowed IRA equipment and the integrity of the centuries old struggle to be mere bargaining chips in their unseemly rush to gain political respectability and acceptability in the eyes of US / British imperialism and unreconstructed Empire Loyalists.

There is no precedent in the history of warfare of any army unilaterally dispensing with its armoury prior to having their aims achieved or at least being in a position that will lead inexorably to an equitable resolution. By their actions Sinn Féin have retrospectively criminalised the struggle for national and social emancipation. It is one thing to call for an end to conflict, as I and other 'dissidents' did long before any ceasefire but it is something else entirely to jettison all of those tents on which we went to war and at the same time criminalise the weaponry that we used[69].

As Bernadette McAliskey said as early as 1994, referring to a Leonard Cohen song, 'the war is over, the good guys lost[70]'. If republicans have been defeated, the modification of the positions of nationalists and unionists within Northern Ireland have been used by Sinn Féin to support the idea that the IRA campaign achieved victory. This interpretation rests upon a revisionist view that the IRA campaign had been the logical extension of the civil rights movement, and that the armed campaign was successful because it led to equality for nationalists within Northern Ireland, to 'parity of esteem' and an 'Ireland of equals'[71]. But as Henry McDonald points out: 'The idea that thousands would have to die and thousands more go to jail or themselves lose their lives so we could have an Irish Language Act or the control of policing and justice powers WITHIN the Northern Ireland state is a gross, deliberate distortion of history[72].' As Bernadette Sands-McKevitt said of her brother: 'Bobby did not die for cross-Border bodies with executive powers. He did not die for nationalists to be equal British citizens within the Northern Ireland state.' She was very critical of key phrases Sinn Féin has championed: 'Words such as "independence" and "freedom" do not seem to be used by any party on this island today. Instead, we have the in-phrases, nice cosy terms like "equal citizenship" and "parity of esteem". Well, the last two IRA volunteers to die on active service...did not die for parity of esteem and equal citizenship. They died for freedom[73].' The republican struggle was about ending British rule, not reforming it on a more equal basis, which led Tommy Gorman to question whether the struggle was worth it[74]. Other republicans critical of the Provisionals such as Brendan Hughes 'do not feel any satisfaction whatsoever. All the questions raised in the course of this struggle have not been answered and the republican struggle has not been concluded'. Asked whether the nationalist middle-class has been the real beneficiary of the armed struggle, Hughes answered: 'Well, it has not been Republicans – apart from those Republicans eager to join that class[75].'

Regarding the strategic failure of Irish republicans, two other important points have to be stressed. First: 'Surrendering honourably is better than holding out to the last. The leaders of the 1916 rising in Dublin chose to surrender rather than subject the city's population to further bloodshed – in politics as in other areas of life it is often necessary to compromise principles.

But there is a gulf between compromise and abandonment that should not be bridged. Otherwise radical ideas and the notion of oppositional currents are devalued. What does it say about the plausibility of the adversarial position if the values espoused in opposition are jetti-soned just to make it into office?'[76] Second, as Brendan Hughes bitterly complained, one must stress the dishonest and immoral way this defeat was organised and sold[77]. As a result of this, the legacy of the peace process for republicanism is not only defeat, but also far more serious, the relinquishing of the moral position of the republican struggle. 'In the process we have lost much of our honesty, sincerity and comradeship,' concluded Brendan Hughes.

Changing the question

As Paddy Hoey puts it:

Perhaps the greatest irony is that Brexit delivered the debate on the border and sovereignty that dissenters had steadfastly clung to for decades, as others believed that a solution to partition would come magically through some kind of evolution of the so-called post-nationalist era. The EU had partly been predicated upon building a structure designed to deal with flare-ups of nationalism which had been at the root cause of continent-wide conflict throughout the nineteenth and early to mid-twentieth centuries, and to nullify the potential for warfare. The civil wars in the former Yugoslavia in the 1990s had galvanised this. However, with Scottish independence, Brexit and its outplaying in Northern Ireland, Catalonia, and upsurges of right-wing sentiment in Hungary, the Netherlands and France, debates about what the nation is, of sovereignty and self-determination were back on the agenda[78].

The fundamental task is to re-engage in these debates and

important questions. Bernadette McAliskey said she wanted to see Irish unity, but not with the present-day administrations in charge. 'Do I think all the people on this minute island would be better off if we had a coherent, single, unitary strategic plan for the economic, social benefit of everyone? Yes I do', she added. But she said that objective couldn't be achieved by absorbing the existing North into the existing South:

> Would I like to see the people having a democratic decision on the context and infrastructure of their government and would I like that to be independent of the British government? Yes, I would. But is that the same thing as having a border poll on 'Would you like to join the Republic?' No it's not. Would I like to dismantle the Irish Republic? Yes. Would I like to dismantle the northern state? Yes.

She added: 'I would like to start again and have a constitutional conference, a series of clear discussions and debates and a democratic process for building a new independent republic in which everybody could feel they belonged.' But she insisted she didn't believe the way to achieve that was as simple as voting in a border poll with a question that didn't relate to the real issues. She didn't know if a border poll would come down – as many people have suggested – to a sectarian headcount, but it would be very difficult to call, she added. 'So the lesson is to stop asking people simplistic questions on complex issues[79].' In 1066 and All That, a popular parody of school history textbooks first published serially in Punch in 1930, it is claimed that William Gladstone 'spent his declining years trying to guess the answer to the Irish Question; unfortunately, whenever he was getting warm, the Irish secretly changed the question'. It seems the imperative now is to change the 'simplistic' question and bring it down to the fundamental conflict between Thomas Paine and Edmund Burke.

In the conclusion to his book on Provisional republicanism, Tommy McKearney writes:

As the Provisional IRA military machine has passed into history and the political party that it generated has drifted into centrism, those continuing to advocate radical Irish republicanism must now review the philosophy's ideological foundations, its practices and its relevance in modern Irish society. This is especially so when other issues exercise the minds of people to a greater extent than the continuation of Partition or the Union. Unemployment, poverty, access to housing, hospitals, education and protection for citizens are of more immediate concern to a majority of the isand's population than is the question of Irish unity[80].

McKearney calls for 'a new and relevant republicanism' to address those issues 'outside establishment republicanism'.

Here, in the context of talks about border polls, it is worth recalling what David Lloyd suggested:

The unity of Ireland in itself is of less value than the transformation of Ireland. This is a project that republicanism shares with labour movements, with radical feminism and with environmental activists, and it is a project that involves the radical rethinking of all our political imaginaries. Rethinking our political ends and strategies will draw on the rich repertoire of alternative social practices in Ireland as well as the dehierarchisation of traditional assumptions and practices. But it will need to draw no less on the practices of decolonisation and the struggles against the New World Order that continue all over the map, among minority communities in the industrial world as in the post-colonial nation-states. These form a network of alternative practices from which we can learn as much by our differences as by our identifications[81].

Key here is the continuing dynamic by which nationalism is formed in articulation with other social movements such as the labour, feminist and environmental movements:

> If the nationalisms with which we are in solidarity are to be emancipatory, rather than fixed on the repressive apparatuses of state formations, it is their conjunctural relation to other social movements that needs to be emphasized and furthered, at both theoretical and practical levels. The possibility of nationalism against the state lies in the recognition of the excess of the people over the nation, and in the understanding that it is, beyond itself, within the very logic of nationalism as a political phenomenon to open and mobilize alternative formations[82].

Last but not least, questioning the unthought axiomatics of Irish republicanism, a product of the philosophic discourse of modernity, should enable one to open up a critical space in which to interrogate Ireland's encounter with modernity itself.

Conclusion: 'Thought as the courage of hopelessness[83]'?

It is interesting to note that this study's conclusions on the Northern Irish peace process are in line with a good number of studies in the field of international relations criticising 'liberal peace' and 'peace processes'[84]. As a discursive object, the concept of 'peace process' is a recent phenomenon. If we take The Times' use of the phrase as an example, it was entirely absent from the paper's journalistic vocabulary until 1974. By 1978, however, the term appeared in 50 articles, and by 1990 562 articles. Since 1990, it has appeared with an average 843 Times articles per year[85]! This reflects the fact that in the field of international relations, 'liberal peace' and 'peace process' have become one of the best means for dominant powers to reconstruct their hegemony. From an emancipatory perspective, one must keep in mind the reality of 'peace building as a colonial practice' and 'peace building as counter-insurgency[86]', as the peace process in Northern Ireland fits these two categories.

Northern Ireland is not insular and follows global trends. The peace process is part of the worldwide crisis of actually existing national liberation movements (ANC, PLO, Sandinistas etc) and the collapse of actually existing socialism[87]. The change in the international balance of forces after the collapse of the soviet bloc put national liberation projects in a position of weakness and forced them to accept unfavourable deals. In the same way that the Republican Movement was associated with the rise of anti-imperialist movements, its evolution also reflects their decline[88]. The peace process and the 1998 Agreement are the Irish equivalent of Francis Fukuyama's 'end of history' thesis[89]. As Perry Anderson put it in 2000:

...the novelty of the present situation stands out in historical view. It can be put like this. For the first time since the Reformation, there are no longer any significant oppositions – that is, systematic rival outlooks – within the thought-world of the West; and scarcely any on a world scale either, if we discount religious doctrines as largely inoperative archaisms...Whatever limitations persist to its practice, neo-liberalism as a set of principles rules undivided across the globe: the most successful ideology in world history[90].

The peace process in Northern Ireland was very much influenced by the 'peace processes' in South Africa and Palestine. The struggles in South Africa, Palestine and Latin America with which republicans identified were in a position of weakness and engaged in peace processes. This encouraged republicans to argue that this was also the way forward in Ireland. Jim Gibney recalls how inspired they were when they saw 'the images of Arafat and Rabin and Mandela and de Klerk' making peace in front of the television cameras[91]. For Edward W. Said however it seemed 'that the media-induced euphoria, to say nothing of official declarations of happiness and satisfaction, belied the grim actuality that the PLO leadership had simply surrendered to Israel[92]'. Close to 25 years after the handshake between Arafat and Rabin on 13 September 1993 and the election of Nelson Mandela as President of South Africa on 27 April 1994, one can see the bitter fruits of the pacification process in Palestine and South Africa, as the massacre of 34 miners in Marikana on 16 August 2012 or the 50 days of the Israeli offensive against Gaza in the summer of 2014 show. The reflections of Frantz Fanon on the 'pitfalls of national consciousness' have never been as relevant. In Ireland as elsewhere, the melancholy of defeat is more appropriate than euphoria for a so-called 'historic opportunity' as the famous U2 'Concert For Yes Vote' performed 19 May 1998 intended to convey.

The peace process is a symptom of a 'thermidorian age[93]' which has witnessed the collapse of historical forces and transformative projects and where historical forces seem exhausted. To paraphrase Walter Benjamin, dialectic is at a standstill. Gramsci: 'The crisis consists precisely in the fact that the old is dying and the new cannot be born.[94]' As Adorno and Horkheimer put it, this work 'is essentially destined to be delivered through the night that is about to fall; it is a kind of message in a bottle', 'it is the surviving message of despair from the shipwrecked[95]'. But to the pessimism of the 'lost cause' and the resignation of the vanquished, Edward W. Said opposes:

the individual intellectual vocation, which is neither disabled by a paralysed sense of political defeat nor impelled by groundless optimism and illusory hope. Consciousness of the possibility of resistance can reside only in the individual will that is fortified by intellectual rigor and an unabated conviction in the need to begin again, with no guarantees except, as Adorno says, the confidence of even the loneliest and most impotent thought that 'what has been cogently thought must be thought in some other place and by other people'. In this way thinking might perhaps acquire and express the momentum of the general, thereby blunting the anguish and despondency of the lost cause, which its enemies have tried to induce. We might well ask from this perspective if any lost cause can ever really be lost[96].

Endnotes

1   Dan Keenan, Recession out of the picture as Fermanagh puts on a brave face for G8 leaders, *Irish Times*, 29 May 2013

2   Lesley-Anne McKeown, Working-class communities 'missed out on Titanic Quarter dividend', Belfast Telegraph, 3 May 2012

3   Henry McDonald, Racially motivated crimes now exceed sectarian ones in Northern Ireland, *The Guardian*, 12 November 2017

4   Quoted in Antonio A. Santucci (2010), *Antonio Gramsci*, New York: Monthly Review Press, 173

5   On this see George Legg (2018) *Northern Ireland and the Politics of Boredom: Conflict, Capital and Culture*, Manchester University Press

6   Jamie Delargy, Vote? Young people in the North don't see the point, *Irish Times*, 9 October 2017

7   Interview with Brendan Hughes, op.cit.

8   John Campbell, Northern Ireland 'was hardest hit' during UK recession, BBC website, 15 July 2014; Mary O'Hara, Stormont chaos set to cause more cuts in Northern Ireland, *The Guardian*, 17 May 2017

9 Paul Cullen, Peace process will survive despite downturn, says McDowell, *Irish Times*, 25 February 2012

10 Boyd Black, Northern Ireland needs the chance to vote Labour, *Belfast Telegraph*, 8 September 2017

11 'Soziologen aber sehen der grimmigen Scherzfrage sich gegenüber: Wo ist das Proletariat?' Theodor W. Adorno, Gesammelte Schriften-Band 4: *Minima Moralia. Reflexionen aus dem beschädigten Leben*, Frankfurt/M: Surhkamp Verlag, 221 (Aphorism 124: Vexierbild)

12 Rebecca Black, We're far more interested in the economy than politics, but most don't trust Stormont to handle it, *Belfast Telegraph*, 7 March 2014

13 Chris Gilligan (2016) Austerity and consociational government in Northern Ireland, *Irish Studies Review*, 24:1, 35-48

14 Quoted in: Daniel Finn, The adaptable Sinn Féin, *Jacobin*, Issue 21, Spring 2016, 101

15 Fredric Jameson (1994), *The Seeds of Time*, New York: Columbia University Press, xii; Slavoj Žižek (ed) (1994), *Mapping Ideology*, London: Verso, 1

16 Michel Houellebecq (2010), *La Carte et le Territoire*, Paris: Flammarion, 397

17 John Newsinger, The Reconstruction of Bourgeois Order in Northern Ireland, *Monthly Review*, 50:2, June 1998, 10-11

18 Frank McNally, An Irishman's Diary, *Irish Times*, 30 September 2017

19 Why Brexit could mean a pricier pint of Guinness, *The Economist*, 15 July 2017

20 Peter Leary, There are three ways out of the Irish border impasse. All are closed to Theresa May, *The Guardian*, 1 March 2018

21 Anton McCabe, NIexit will reduce protection, *Village Magazine*, 19 April 2018

22 Suzanne Breen, Brexit scaremongering chorus grows,

Belfast Telegraph, 27 April 2018

23 Simon Carswell, Ex-IRA Men: 'United Ireland?' It's all guff', *Irish Times*, 8 April 2017

24 Gerry Moriarty, Brexit campaign in North 'played on racism and emotions', *Irish Times*, 1 July 2016

25 Étienne Balibar, Le Brexit, cet anti-Grexit, *Libération*, 27 Juin 2016

26 Gareth Gordon, Unionist MP Lady Sylvia Hermon expects to see border poll, BBC website, 3 May 2018

27 Scottish referendum: Sinn Féin's Martin McGuinness calls for Northern Ireland border poll following Scotland result, *Belfast Telegraph*, 19 September 2014, Sinn Féin calls for border poll on united Ireland after Brexit win in EU referendum, *Belfast Telegraph* 24 June 2016, Sinn Féin urges unity referendum within five years, *Irish Times*, 2 April 2018

28 John Manley, Nationalist anger at Varadkar '50 plus one' remarks, *Irish News*, 18 October 2017, Laurence White, 51 per cent majority not enough for Irish unity: Ahern, *Belfast Telegraph*, 20 November 2008

29 Paul Nolan, United Ireland may be in the gift of 'others', *Irish Times*, 19 June 2018

30 Dr Éamon Phoenix, Unionism shocked to the core, *Irish News*, 6 March 2017

31 Constitutional Preference - What do you think the long-term policy for Northern Ireland should be? Northern Ireland Life and Times Survey: Political Attitudes, www.ark.ac.uk/nilt/results/polatt.html

32 Twenty years after a peace deal the mood is sour in Northern Ireland. *The Economist*, 31 March 2018

33 Paul Nolan, United Ireland may be in the gift of 'others', op.cit.

34 Jonathan Bell, Most people in Northern Ireland don't want border poll: Prime Minister Theresa May, *Belfast Telegraph*,

15 May 2018

35 Bernadette McAliskey: 'Sinn Féin's talk of border poll is game-play, it doesn't want united Ireland it can't control', *Belfast Telegraph*, 15 March 2017

36 We believe, with Pearse: 'As long as Ireland is unfree the only honourable attitude for Irishmen and Irish women is an attitide of revolt', *Saoirse*, December 2013

37 Let us leave behind the failure and mediocrity of the past and set our sights firmly on the bright horizon of a new dawn for the Irish nation, *Saoirse*, December 2014

38 We are the true heirs to a proud and noble revolutionary tradition, *Saoirse*, November 2017

39 See the forthcoming book by Marisa McGlinchey and Kevin Bean (2019) *The Politics and Ideology of 'Dissident' Irish Republicanism: Standing by the Republic*, Manchester University Press; Paddy Hoey (2018) *Shinners, Dissos and Dissenters: Irish republican media activism since the Good Friday Agreement*, Manchester University Press, 45-84; Kevin Bean (2012) 'New dissidents are but old Provisionals writ large'? The Dynamics of Dissident Republicanism in the New Northern Ireland, The Political Quarterly, 83:2, 210-218

40 Tony Crowley (2011) 'Dissident': A Brief Note, Critical Quarterly, 53:2, 1-11

41 Eamonn McCann, Passive support for 'dissident' Republicans, The Derry Journal, 16 February 2010

42 See in particular: Liam Clarke, Four months before a car blew up in Omagh, the gardai and MI5 were told it would be there. Why did they do nothing? Sunday Times, 26 February 2006; Colm Heatley, Omagh: The Questions that still need answering, Sunday Business Post, 12 August 2007, Colm Heatley, Omagh Bomb trial described as 'farce' by victim's husband, ibid, Liam Clarke, Secret service in dock over Omagh, Sunday Times, 21 September 2008, John

Ware, The words that might have saved Omagh, Sunday Telegraph, 14 September 2008, John Ware, Omagh bombing inquiry must reveal the truth about GCHQ intercepts, Sunday Telegraph, 21 September 2008

43   Editorial, An Larc: the Voice of Cogús Republican Prisoners, Easter 2018, 2

44   Jocelyn Evans and Jonathan Tonge (2012) Menace Without Mandate? Is There Any Sympathy for 'Dissident' Irish Republicanism in Northern Ireland? *Terrorism and Political Violence*, 24:1, 61-78

45   James Connolly, *Collected Works – Volume Two*, Dublin: New Books, 1988, 177

46   Robin Wilson (2016), op.cit., 46

47   Barry McCaffrey, RIRA 'war' must end says senior dissident, Irish News, 14 October 2005

48   Paul Bew (2007), *Ireland: The Politics of Enmity 1789-2006*, Oxford: Oxford University Press, 68-70

49   Henry McDonald, Catholics main victims of Northern Ireland republican terror groups, *The Guardian*, 28 April 2016

50   Ronnie Munck (1984) Repression, Insurgency, and Popular Justice: The Irish Case, *Crime and Social Justice*, 21-22, 81-94; Ronnie Munck (1988), The Lads and the Hoods: Alternative Justice in an Irish Context, in M. Tomlinson, T. Varley, and C. McCullagh (eds.) (1988), Whose Law and Order? Aspects of Crime and Social Control in Irish Society, Belfast: Sociological Association, 41-53

51   A Necessary Evil?, *Scairt Amach: The Voice of Republican Prisoners*, Issue 4, Summer 2015, 14-15

52   Paddy Hoey (2018), 66

53   In the same place, 21-22 and 111-141

54   2,400 lives saved in Northern Ireland by ending of the Troubles, Belfast Telegraph, 11 April 2018

55   Paul Nolan (2012), op.cit., 15

56   Ralf Sotscheck (1999), Interview with Bernadette McAliskey, 6 April 1999, in: Dietrich Schulze Marmeling, Hans-Christian Oeser, Jörg Rademacher, Jürgen Schneider (Hg.), *Irland Almanach 1 - Krieg und Frieden*, Munster: Unrast Verlag

57   Eamonn McCann, Cynic me says welfare row has been a put-up job, *Belfast Telegraph*, 3 June 2015

58   Jonathan Freedland, Whatever Gerry Adams' past, peace takes precedence over justice, *Guardian*, 3 May 2014

59   On the concept of 'just peace' see: Edward W. Said (2006), A method for thinking about just peace, in Pierre Allan and Alexis Keller (eds), *What is a Just Peace?* Oxford University Press, 176-195

60   Henry McDonald, Peace and poverty for Troubles survivors, *The Guardian*, 29 August 2014

61   Ciarán Hancock, Brexit shines harsh light on North's economy, *Irish Times*, 22 March 2017

62   Robbie McVeigh (1998), The British/Irish 'Peace Process' and the Colonial Legacy, op.cit., 52

63   Edward W. Said (1994), *Representations of the Intellectual*, London: Vintage, 75, 81

64   Bernadette McAliskey, speech to Clár na mBan conference 12 March 1994, in: Angela Bourke et.al. (eds) (2002) *The Field Day anthology of Irish writing, vol. 5: Irish women's writings and traditions.*, Cork: Cork University Press, 420-423

65   Chris Gilligan (1997), Peace or Pacification Process? A brief critique of the peace process, in Chris Gilligan and Jonathan Tonge (eds), *Peace or War? Understanding the Peace Process in Northern Ireland*, Aldershot: Ashgate, 19-34

66   The idea of 'simulation of peace' is taken from: Jan Selby (2011), The Political Economy of Peace Processes, in: Michael Pugh, Neil Cooper, Mandy Turner (eds), *Whose Peace? Critical Perspectives on the Political Economy of Peacebuilding*, Basingstoke: Palgrave Macmillan, 27

67 Ralf Sotscheck, Interview with Bernadette McAliskey, 6 April 1999, op.cit.

68 Anthony McIntyre, By shaking the Queen's hand, Martin McGuinness accepts her sovereignty, *The Guardian*, 26 June 2012

69 Tommy Gorman, Dropping the last veil, *The Blanket* website, 23 November 2004

70 Anthony McIntyre (2008), *Good Friday: The Death of Irish Republicanism*, New York: Ausubo Press, 226

71 For a polemic against this idea see: Henry McDonald (2009), *Gunsmoke and Mirrors: How Sinn Féin Dressed up Defeat as Victory*, Dublin: Gill & Macmillan

72 Henry McDonald, How the Provos 'sold out', *Belfast Telegraph*, 19 November 2008

73 Suzanne Breen, Sister of hunger-striker denounces peace process as deception, *Irish Times*, 8 January 1998. See also: Bimpe Archer, Sister of Bobby Sands denounces former comrades at mother's funeral, *Irish News*, 16 January 2018

74 Tommy Gorman, Was it all for nothing? *Andersonstown News*, 11 September 1999

75 Interview with Brendan Hughes, op.cit.

76 Anthony McIntyre, By shaking the Queen's hand, Martin McGuinness accepts her sovereignty, op.cit.

77 Ed Moloney (2010), *Voices From the Grave: Two Men's War in Ireland*, London: Faber and Faber, 292. For more background on this issue see: Ed Moloney (2007), *A Secret History of the IRA*, London: Allen Lane The Penguin Press, second revised and updated edition

78 Paddy Hoey (2018), op.cit., 178

79 Bernadette McAliskey: 'Sinn Féin's talk of border poll is game-play, it doesn't want united Ireland it can't control', op.cit.

80 Tommy McKearney (2011), *The Provisional IRA: From Insurrection to Parliament*, London: Pluto Press, 207

81 David Lloyd, *Ireland After History*, University of Notre Dame Press in association with Field Day, 107-108

82 In the same place, 36

83 Le philosophe Giorgio Agamben: 'La pensée, c'est le courage du désespoir'. http://www.telerama.fr/idees/le-philosophe-giorgio-agamben-la-pensee-c-est-le-courage-du-desespoir,78653.php

84 Jan Selby (2013), The myth of liberal peace-building, *Conflict, Security & Development*, 13:1, 57-86 for an overview of the main theses of this current

85 Jan Selby (2008), Peace Processes: A Genealogy and Critique, Department of International Relations – University of Sussex, Presentation 7 January 2008, 2 and 5. Available here: https://www.sussex.ac.uk/webteam/gateway/file.php?name=rip-peace-processes&site=12

86 For the concept of peacebuilidng as colonial practice and counter-insurgency in the case of Palestine for example see: Mandy Turner (2012), Completing the Circle: Peacebuilding as Colonial Practice in the Occupied Palestinian Territory, *International Peacekeeping*, 19:4, 492-507 and Mandy Turner (2015), Peacebuilding as Counterinsurgency in the Occupied Palestinian Territory, *Review of International Studies*, 41:1, 73-98

87 Michael Cox (1997). Bringing in the 'International': The IRA Ceasefire and the End of the Cold War, *International Affairs*, 73:4, 671-693

88 Mark Ryan (1994), *War & Peace in Ireland: Britain and the IRA in the New World Order*, London: Pluto Press, 30-43

89 Arthur Aughey (1998). Fukuyama, the End of History and the Irish Question, *Irish Studies in International Affairs*,9, 85-92

90 Perry Anderson: Renewals. *New Left Review*, January-February 2000, 17

91 Jim Gibney, Making headlines around the world for right

reasons, *Irish News*, 5 April 2007

92   Edward W. Said, *Representations of the Intellectual*, op.cit., 81

93   Steven Corcoran (2015), *The Badiou Dictionary*, Edinburgh University Press, 353-358. The Thermidorian reaction to the French Revolution began on 9 Thermidor Year 2 (1794) marked by the putting to death of Robespierre and Saint-Just. To put it in Saint-Just' terms, 'What do those who want neither Virtue nor Terror really want?' His answer: the end of revolution and the restoration of the order of proprietors. It is a counter-revolutionary period.

94   Antonio Gramsci, *Selections from the Prison Notebooks*, London: Lawrence & Wishart, 1971, 276

95   Horkheimer Letter to Salka Viertel, 29 June 1940, Max Horkheimer, Gesammelte Schriften-Band 16: *Briefwechsel 1937-1940*, Frankfurt:M: S. Fischer Verlage, 726. The English translation of: 'It is the surviving message of despair from the shipwrecked' is not quite the German original 'Sie ist die wahre Flaschenpost' which would translate as 'it is the authentic message in a bottle'. Theodor W. Adorno, Gesammelte Schriften-Band 12: *Philosophie der neuen Musik*, Frankfurt/M: Surhkamp Verlag, 126

96   Edward W. Said (2000), On Lost Causes, in: *Reflections on Exile and Other Essays*, Cambridge, Harvard University Press, 553

CULTURE, SOCIETY & POLITICS

Contemporary culture has eliminated the concept and public figure of the intellectual. A cretinous anti-intellectualism presides, cheer-led by hacks in the pay of multinational corporations who reassure their bored readers that there is no need to rouse themselves from their stupor. Zer0 Books knows that another kind of discourse – intellectual without being academic, popular without being populist – is not only possible: it is already flourishing. Zer0 is convinced that in the unthinking, blandly consensual culture in which we live, critical and engaged theoretical reflection is more important than ever before.

If you have enjoyed this book, why not tell other readers by posting a review on your preferred book site.

Recent bestsellers from Zero Books are:

In the Dust of This Planet
Horror of Philosophy vol. 1
Eugene Thacker
In the first of a series of three books on the Horror of
Philosophy, *In the Dust of This Planet* offers the genre of horror
as a way of thinking about the unthinkable.
Paperback: 978-1-84694-676-9 ebook: 978-1-78099-010-1

Capitalist Realism
Is there no alternative?
Mark Fisher
An analysis of the ways in which capitalism has presented itself
as the only realistic political-economic system.
Paperback: 978-1-84694-317-1 ebook: 978-1-78099-734-6

Rebel Rebel
Chris O'Leary
David Bowie: every single song. Everything you want to know,
everything you didn't know.
Paperback: 978-1-78099-244-0 ebook: 978-1-78099-713-1

Cartographies of the Absolute
Alberto Toscano, Jeff Kinkle
An aesthetics of the economy for the twenty-first century.
Paperback: 978-1-78099-275-4 ebook: 978-1-78279-973-3

Malign Velocities
Accelerationism and Capitalism
Benjamin Noys

Long listed for the Bread and Roses Prize 2015, *Malign Velocities* argues against the need for speed, tracking acceleration as the symptom of the ongoing crises of capitalism.

Paperback: 978-1-78279-300-7 ebook: 978-1-78279-299-4

Meat Market
Female Flesh under Capitalism
Laurie Penny

A feminist dissection of women's bodies as the fleshy fulcrum of capitalist cannibalism, whereby women are both consumers and consumed.

Paperback: 978-1-84694-521-2 ebook: 978-1-84694-782-7

Poor but Sexy
Culture Clashes in Europe East and West
Agata Pyzik

How the East stayed East and the West stayed West.

Paperback: 978-1-78099-394-2 ebook: 978-1-78099-395-9

Romeo and Juliet in Palestine
Teaching Under Occupation
Tom Sperlinger

Life in the West Bank, the nature of pedagogy and the role of a university under occupation.

Paperback: 978-1-78279-637-4 ebook: 978-1-78279-636-7

Sweetening the Pill
or How We Got Hooked on Hormonal Birth Control
Holly Grigg-Spall
Has contraception liberated or oppressed women? *Sweetening the Pill* breaks the silence on the dark side of hormonal contraception.
Paperback: 978-1-78099-607-3 ebook: 978-1-78099-608-0

Why Are We The Good Guys?
Reclaiming Your Mind from the Delusions of Propaganda
David Cromwell
A provocative challenge to the standard ideology that Western power is a benevolent force in the world.
Paperback: 978-1-78099-365-2 ebook: 978-1-78099-366-9

Readers of ebooks can buy or view any of these bestsellers by clicking on the live link in the title. Most titles are published in paperback and as an ebook. Paperbacks are available in traditional bookshops. Both print and ebook formats are available online.

Find more titles and sign up to our readers' newsletter at http://www.johnhuntpublishing.com/culture-and-politics

Follow us on Facebook
at https://www.facebook.com/ZeroBooks

and Twitter at https://twitter.com/Zer0Books